THE
PROPHET
AND HIS
MESSAGE

THE
PROPHET
AND HIS
MESSAGE

READING OLD TESTAMENT

PROPHECY TODAY

MICHAEL J. WILLIAMS

P.O. BOX 817 • PHILLIPSBURG • NEW JERSEY 08865-0817

Italics within Scripture quotations indicate emphasis added.

Page design by Lakeside Design Plus
Typesetting by Michelle Feaster

Printed in the United States of America

Library of Congress Cataloging-in-Publication Data

Williams, Michael James, 1956–
    The prophet and his message : reading Old Testament prophecy today / Michael J. Williams.
      p. cm.
    Includes bibliographical references and indexes.
    ISBN 0-87552-555-5 (pbk.)
    1. Bible. O.T. Prophets—Criticism, interpretation, etc. I. Title.

BS1505.52.W55 2003
220.1'5—dc21
                          2003054941

CONTENTS

PREFACE

This book is partly the fruit of several years of teaching and discussion with students and faculty at Calvin Theological Seminary in Grand Rapids, Michigan. The eager, insightful, and committed students at this Reformed institution made it clear to me that some comprehensive and coherent explanation of the continuing relevance and contemporary significance of the Old Testament from a Reformed perspective needed further explication. My gifted fellow professors, who unselfishly gave their time, thoughts, and advice, greatly assisted me in this attempt at such an exposition. Although we are a collegial bunch and work closely together toward advancing the cause of Jesus Christ in the world, I am sure that at least some of my particular perspectives in this book will not find unanimous endorsement among them.

The other main contributing factor that led to this present work is my experience in Reformed churches. Countless sermons, Bible studies, adult education classes, and conversations with parishioners all have convinced me that there exists within the church a general lack of understanding about how to deal with the Old Testament. It has been my goal in this book to provide some guidance for interested laypersons, as well as those who are embarking on vocations that require them to think more deeply about such things, on how to approach the entire Old Testament from a prophetic perspective. While my success in achieving this goal must be decided by the reader, I am confident that I have provided at least the basis for healthy, productive conversation in this area.

The possibility for physically accomplishing this project was provided in large part by a generous grant from the Wabash Center for Teaching and Learning in Theology and Religion in Crawfordsville, Indiana. Their enormous efforts on behalf of religious education are widely unrecognized, but are nevertheless widely felt.

I must also acknowledge the gracious beneficence of the board of trustees of Calvin Theological Seminary, who provided me with a sabbatical within which I was able to complete the bulk of the research and writing.

Finally, I want to express my deep appreciation for the tireless assistance and faithful support of my wife Dawn, who patiently read every word of the manuscript. It and I certainly owe her an enormous debt of gratitude for her attentive and caring treatment.

ABBREVIATIONS

ANET	*Ancient Near Eastern Texts Relating to the Old Testament*
CAD	*The Assyrian Dictionary of the Oriental Institute of the University of Chicago*
EDT	*Evangelical Dictionary of Theology*
EuroJTh	*European Journal of Theology*
HTR	*Harvard Theological Review*
IDB	*Interpreter's Dictionary of the Bible*
JBL	*Journal of Biblical Literature*
JSOT	*Journal for the Study of the Old Testament*
JSOTSup	*Journal for the Study of the Old Testament, Supplement Series*
NIDOTTE	*New International Dictionary of Old Testament Theology and Exegesis*
OTL	Old Testament Library
TDOT	*Theological Dictionary of the Old Testament*
TLOT	*Theological Lexicon of the Old Testament*
VT	*Vetus Testamentum*
VTSup	Supplements to *Vetus Testamentum*
WTJ	*Westminster Theological Journal*
ZAW	*Zeitschrift für Alttestamenliche Wissenschaft*

INTRODUCTION

A new pastime is gaining popularity among people who have time and money on their hands, but are dissatisfied with the usual slate of vacation and recreational options. Perhaps uneasy with their ignorance of other cultures, or simply curious, vacationers are willingly handing over large amounts of money to participate in "adventure travel." These exotic expeditions are designed to awaken participants to patterns of life in places far beyond their comfort zones. "Adventure travel" describes

> travel patterns that take Western people into what are essentially non-Western, geographically remote places. . . . [It] includes both the natural and cultural systems of the visited place. Moreover, adventure travel usually is linked to some thematic form of travel—safaris, trekking, kayaking, and in many cases simply local public transportation—which can be adventure enough for those coming from the industrial, convenience-oriented societies of the Western world.[1]

1. David Zurick, *Errant Journeys: Adventure Travel in a Modern Age* (Austin: University of Texas Press, 1995), 10.

1

Most contemporary readers of the Bible probably never realize that they are embarking on a sort of "adventure travel" all their own. Our "thematic form of travel" is essentially reading, and through our reading we encounter an ancient and often mysterious world of foreign and harsh geography, strange and unfamiliar customs and practices, and peoples for whom religion was not conceptually compartmentalized, but interwoven into the fabric of everyday life.

To maximize the benefit of our journey into this foreign environment, we must sensitize ourselves to the subtleties of the biblical world and acquaint ourselves with its various features on its own terms. Steve Conlon elaborates on the responsibilities of the adventure traveler:

> The Art of Adventure Travel involves seeing beyond the new environment's surface, using all of your senses to connect with the essence of a place. . . . It means listening, with your inner ear, to the sounds of a place: the yak bells, the mother calling her child, the monk chanting, the wind whispering. . . . It means sitting in a tea shop, or wherever, and looking into the eyes and spirit of a fellow human being, and marveling at the similarity of people and the diversity of the human race. It means stretching your mind and imagination as well as your legs, and coming home a little richer than you left.[2]

It may take us a little time and effort to accomplish these goals during our reading excursion into the biblical texts. It may mean that we might have to jettison some of our pre-

2. Steve Conlon, "The Art of Adventure Travel," in the 1990–91 catalog of the Above the Clouds Trekking Agency (P.O. Box 398, Worcester, MA 01602), p. 2, cited by Zurick, *Errant Journeys*, 135–36.

conceptions and tune our ear to hear the voices of the biblical passages themselves. It certainly means that we will have to proceed slowly and carefully to ensure that we learn as much as possible during our stay in this foreign literary culture that we have come to visit.

Though the difficulty of comprehendingly encountering the foreign biblical culture is formidable, this task is significantly compounded when we focus our attention upon the Old Testament prophets.[3] Of all the characters in the Old Testament, the prophets are probably the most unusual and the most mysterious—and they were already recognized as such in their own day and by their own people! Just imagine the reaction of the local populace to a naked Isaiah running around in their midst (Isa. 20), or to a yoked Jeremiah (Jer. 27), or to the freshly shaved head of Ezekiel (Ezek. 5)! In addition to such bizarre behavior, the biblical prophets are also associated with fantastic visions, wonderful miracles, passionate discourses, extreme emotions, and both clear and vague pronouncements concerning the future. Robert R. Wilson notes: "Prophets have always been surrounded by an aura of mystery. Because they are intermediaries between the divine and human worlds, prophets appear to their hearers as terrifying yet magnetic and fascinating figures."[4] Before we begin to examine their messages, we need to come to some understanding of these enigmatic personalities.

---

3. I will be using the terms "Old Testament prophets" and "biblical prophets" purposely to avoid any confusion of these figures with their contemporary counterparts in the ancient Near East. While there are certainly areas of overlap between these two groups, and we can gain some understanding of the former by giving attention to the latter, they are fundamentally different. This radical difference is that the biblical prophets alone are singled out by the only true God to accomplish his purposes among his people.

4. Robert R. Wilson, "Early Israelite Prophecy," in James L. Mays and Paul J. Achtemeier, eds., *Interpreting the Prophets* (Philadelphia: Fortress, 1987), 1.

The biblical prophets encompass a rather large group of characters, including both men and women, who come from a variety of walks of life. They include the well-known writing prophets, who have given their names to biblical books, but also include less familiar, even obscure, figures. While some of these less well known figures are named in the text, we know very little else about them. Consider, for example, the brief biblical mentions of Ahijah (1 Kings 11:29–39), Shemaiah (1 Kings 12:22–24), and Hulda (2 Kings 22:14–20). We even know some of the words and actions of several prophets who are not even provided with names in the text, such as those mentioned in Judges 6:7–10; 1 Samuel 10:10–13; 19:18–24; and 1 Kings 18:4 (where reference is made to a hundred unnamed prophets). How are we to understand such a diverse collection of characters and characteristics?

While many contemporary books are dedicated to explicating the messages of the writing prophets, not much study has been done of a more comprehensive nature. What we seek to do in this book is come to some understanding of what the prophets are all about. What makes a person a prophet? What, exactly, should we understand the essential function(s) of the prophet to be? And how do they carry out their function(s)? These are critical questions and deserve some careful consideration.

If we are ever to arrive at a secure understanding of any individual prophet and his[5] message, we must first be sure that we are aware of the larger framework within which that prophet is conducting his ministry. What should we look for? Many years ago Egyptian hieroglyphs presented a seemingly

5. While there are also female prophets in the Old Testament (for a discussion of these, see Hobart E. Freeman, *An Introduction to the Old Testament Prophets* [Chicago: Moody, 1968], 35–36), for simple convenience I will be using the masculine pronoun to refer to an individual prophet.

insoluble riddle to scholars who sought to understand the message communicated by those strange shapes and figures. Not until the discovery of the Rosetta Stone, which provided the translation of those shapes and figures into a known language, did the linguistic knot become untied. That is the way it is with the prophets. Without some sort of key for understanding not only what but also how they are communicating, their messages are in danger of being largely indecipherable or misinterpreted.

This interpretive danger has often resulted in the distortion of prophetic messages into proofs of the interpreter's particular theology. The biblical prophets seem particularly susceptible to having attributed to them all sorts of odd and fanciful ideas, especially concerning the future. They have been credited with forecasting everything from the precise date for the end of the world to the specific details of its demise. Besides being contrary to Scripture, such abuse of the prophets for Armageddon calculations not only results in embarrassment when those calculations prove incorrect, but also presumes that the role of the prophet is primarily that of predictor—a presumption, as we will see, that needs to be carefully examined. We find such fanciful, though popular, exegesis of biblical prophecy in works such as those by Hal Lindsey.[6] This dangerous practice of jumping to unwarranted or at least highly speculative conclusions about the fulfillment of biblical prophecy can be averted by a prior careful consideration of what a "prophet" is and what he is supposed to accomplish.

A final danger that we want to avoid is one that unfortunately often threatens our churches and religious schools. It begins with a legitimate and prudent realization of the difficulty involved in correctly understanding the biblical

---

6. Hal Lindsey, *The Late Great Planet Earth* (Grand Rapids: Zondervan, 1970).

prophets, but is ultimately unwisely resolved by a simple avoidance of them. It is rare that one hears a sermon from the prophetic books today.[7] Even in educational settings, teaching concerning the prophets is often restricted to introductory matters or surveys of the content of individual prophetic books, without substantive or comprehensive biblical-theological exposition of their messages. The primary reason pulpits and classrooms neglect the prophets is the simple fact that most people do not feel equipped to deal with them. Lacking a comprehensive, "big-picture" perspective on the prophets as a whole results in an understandable difficulty in comprehending the role of any individual prophet within God's redemptive revelation and continuing redemptive activity. We need to step back from a narrow concentration on specific individual prophets or specific functions of the prophetic ministry in order to gain a much broader perspective of the defining characteristics of the biblical prophets as a whole and the role they play in God's redemptive program. Only then will we be in a position to grasp the significance of the contributions of individual prophets as well.

The point of view we will be taking in our comprehensive and focused analysis—indeed a standpoint that makes such an analysis possible at all—is a Reformed perspective of Scripture. This perspective involves some fundamental presuppositions that intellectual honesty demands I set forth before we begin our study.

---

7. It is rare to hear a sermon from *anywhere* in the Old Testament today (except for the occasional psalm). Sidney Greidanus, *Preaching Christ from the Old Testament: A Contemporary Hermeneutical Method* (Grand Rapids: Eerdmans, 1999), 16–25, lists four reasons for this general neglect: (1) the New Testament weighting of lectionaries; (2) the negative effect of critical Old Testament scholarship; (3) the outright rejection of the Old Testament for various reasons; and (4) historical-cultural, theological, ethical, and practical difficulties with preaching from the Old Testament.

Perhaps the most important of these presuppositions is the conviction of the all-encompassing sovereignty of God. As we take careful note of the details of what Scripture records for us, it is my presupposition that every aspect of what we observe is intended, directed, and effectuated by our sovereign Lord: the prophetic call, the reception of the prophetic message, the content of the prophetic message and its mode of delivery, the way the prophetic message is received by those who hear it, the specific form the prophet's words and biographical information take in the recorded word, the realization of the prophetic message throughout time, and the providential delivery of the written record of the prophet's words and life to us. Far from a disjointed chain of unrelated circumstances that can be studied individually in an objectively detached fashion, these details, I maintain, are all under the sovereign control of God, who has preserved them in Scripture and directs them toward their appointed end (Isa. 55:10–11).[8] Our response to the prophetic message is nothing less than a response to divinely intended and directed communication, and therefore has eternal consequences for each one of us.

Another aspect of the Reformed perspective affecting our study of the prophets is its assertion of the organic nature of Scripture. By this we mean that there is no essential difference in character between the Old Testament and the New Testament. Each is inspired by God, who by the Holy Spirit moved holy men of old to write divine words in their own style (2 Peter 1:20–21). The redemptive revelation grows over time as an organic entity. It develops and unfolds,

8. This aspect of God's sovereignty extensively overlaps the concept of his providence, defined as "that continued exercise of the divine energy whereby the Creator preserves all his creatures, is operative in all that comes to pass in the world, and directs all things to their appointed end" (Louis Berkhof, *Systematic Theology*, 4th ed. [Grand Rapids: Eerdmans, 1941], 166).

but does not radically change in its essential nature or purpose.[9] It is here that we part company with theologies that regard God as behaving one way toward humankind in one testament, and another way in the other testament. We maintain, instead, that God is consistent in his interaction with human beings and has been communicating the same redemptive message in various ways throughout human history.

Another important aspect of the Reformed perspective is simply that all of redemptive revelation finds its focus in the culminating redemptive work of Jesus Christ. All of the Old Testament points forward to him, and all of the New Testament reflects back on the significance of the Christ event.[10]

Finally, because of the Reformed conviction that our world belongs to God, and because of our firm belief that we have the responsibility to be God's agents of reconciliation in the world (2 Cor. 5:18–20), we are led inescapably to the conclusion that we, as Christians, are called to active involvement and interaction with the unbelieving world for Christ's sake. What form should this take? How can we be certain that our own pet concerns are not eclipsing or distorting our scripturally based responsibilities? By focusing our attention on the prophets, we will be able to answer

9. Willem A. VanGemeren, *Interpreting the Prophetic Word: An Introduction to the Prophetic Literature of the Old Testament* (Grand Rapids: Zondervan, 1990), 46: "The progressive revelation of God is like a seed that germinates, grows, and develops. . . . The organic and progressive message of the prophets is inner-related, distinct, full of movement, diverse, but always revealing an inner unity, being bound together by one Spirit and disclosing one plan of redemption."

10. Louis Berkhof, *Principles of Biblical Interpretation* (Grand Rapids: Baker, 1950), 142: "All the facts of the redemptive history that is recorded in the Bible center in that great fact [i.e., the redemptive act of God in Jesus Christ]. The various lines of the Old Testament revelation converge towards it, and those of the New Testament revelation radiate from it. It is only in their binding center, Jesus Christ, that the narratives of Scripture find their explanation. The interpreter will truly understand them only insofar as he discerns their connection with the great central fact of Sacred History."

these and other questions with confidence because the prophets too addressed their culture amid a myriad of concerns and distractions present in their day. The message they communicated and how they communicated it are still vitally important as guides for the church today.

Because of this continuing importance to believers, and because of the dangers we face if we simply ignore the prophets or interpret them incorrectly, we must proceed carefully and systematically in our study if we are to understand correctly the biblical prophets and what they are doing, or, more precisely, what God is doing through them. To this end, let us briefly note a few principles underlying the methodology followed in this volume.

First, the prophetic writings comprise a substantial portion of Scripture; and, as we read in 2 Timothy 3:16, *"All Scripture is God-breathed and is useful for teaching, rebuking, correcting and training in righteousness."* To benefit from the prophetic portions of Scripture, we cannot ignore them. In fact, I hope to demonstrate that far from being a tedious exercise, studying the prophets opens a window through which, if we look carefully enough, we may glimpse the entirety of God's redemptive plan.[11] Indeed, the church itself is "built on the foundation of the apostles and prophets" (Eph. 2:20).

While such claims may seem to be hyperbolic and promise a little too much, the importance of correctly understanding the prophets can hardly be overstated. In Amos 3:7 we find a remarkable passage that states: "Surely the Sovereign LORD does nothing without revealing his plan to his ser-

---

11. Freeman, *Introduction to the Old Testament Prophets*, 11: "The religion and history of Israel are fundamentally prophetic. The Old Testament revelation was, according to Hebrews 1:1, a revelation through the prophets"; and VanGemeren, *Interpreting the Prophetic Word*, 18: "The prophets opened windows to the grand plan of God by which the eye of hope may have a vision of what God has prepared for his people."

vants the prophets." This is an amazing statement with profound implications. It suggests that spending some time studying "his servants the prophets" holds the promise of yielding insight into everything that God does. Surely no better motivation exists for anyone interested in understanding God's special revelation and redemptive activity than such a promise as this.

Yet before we can focus our attention on the prophets and their messages, we have to know what we're looking for. Therefore, in the first two chapters, we will consider the fundamental question of what a prophet is. While this may seem like a simple question and one for which we all may have developed personally satisfying answers over the years, historically the question of what the prophets are has been answered in a wide variety of ways. Acknowledging the groundwork of many skilled researchers who have preceded us, we will examine their scholarly contributions for any help they may give us in our efforts to understand the essential nature of a prophet. Weighing these insights against the biblical data, we will subsequently develop a definition of a prophet that is wide enough to account for all of the information we have obtained and that may serve as a beginning point for our subsequent investigation.

Second, we study the biblical prophets to gain insight into one of the three offices of the Old Testament—the other two being the priestly office and the kingly office. I use the term "office" here in a formal sense to mean a distinct position of leadership among the people of God to which certain specific duties and expectations are attached.[12] In the Old

12. The report (Report 44) on "Ecclesiastical Office and Ordination" prepared by a study committee of the Christian Reformed Church and found in its *Agenda for Synod* (1973), 501–82, describes those occupying the Old Testament offices of prophet, priest, and king as "the necessary functionaries to aid in the nurturing, correction, and regulation of the life of the covenantal community" (p. 518).

Testament, the prophets as well as the priests and kings were anointed with oil;[13] that is, they were publicly designated as set aside by God for a special purpose.[14] It does us little good, however, simply to be aware of the prophetic office without having any comprehension of what it entails.[15] We study the prophetic office not only to expand our understanding of one of the three main emphases of the Old Testament, but also (as we will come to appreciate more fully later) to prepare ourselves to recognize the parameters of this office in later redemptive history, in Israel/Judah, in Jesus Christ, and finally in the church today. Therefore, in the third chapter we shift our focus slightly and concentrate more specifically on a functional description of a prophet. That is, we will ask the question What does a prophet do? In this chapter we will begin to bring into focus three general emphases or directions of the prophetic task. These will be developed following the biblical texts and will further enhance our subsequent investigation from a practical perspective.

Third, the functional understanding of the prophetic ministry leads to another benefit of studying the biblical prophets. Once we understand the general outline of the prophetic task, we will be able to recognize when it is being deliberately carried out. This applies not just to individuals, but also to communities that behave as corporate personalities. In the fourth chapter, therefore, we will use the outline of the prophetic task that we have distilled to consider the

13. See, for example, 1 Kings 19:16 and Isa. 61:1.

14. John Van Engen, "Anoint, Anointing," in *Evangelical Dictionary of Theology*, ed. Walter A. Elwell (Grand Rapids: Baker, 1984), 51–52.

15. John Calvin, *Institutes of the Christian Religion*, ed. John T. McNeill, trans. Ford Lewis Battles (Philadelphia: Westminster, 1960), 2.15.1 (p. 494): "Yet it would be of little value to know these [offices] without understanding their purpose and use."

question of whether the prophetic task belongs not only to individual biblical prophets, but also to the nation of Israel/Judah as a corporate personality. When viewed from a prophetic perspective, the redemptive history of Israel/Judah becomes far more revelatory. Reflecting on the prophetic role of Israel/Judah will enable us to grasp the role of this nation in God's redemptive plan and will give us a perspective from which to view the entire Old Testament.

Fourth, an appreciation of the prophets and their functions also enables us to understand the ministry of Jesus Christ more comprehensively. For Jesus not only fulfills prophecy, but also perfectly fulfills the prophetic office. It would be extremely difficult to understand the person and work of Christ without understanding the prophetic office. Conversely, because all of redemptive revelation finds its fulfillment and focus in Jesus Christ, we must check our understanding of prophets and the prophetic task by looking for their fulfillment in him. If our conclusions are correct, we will find our definition of a prophet and our outline of prophetic functions fulfilled in the person and work of Christ. Moreover, the fulfillment that we find will not simply consist of a recognition of the presence of certain elements, but we must find *all* of the elements carried to a point of ultimate realization—that is, *perfectly fulfilled*—in Christ. In the fifth chapter, therefore, we focus our attention on this true light foreshadowed in the Old Testament to check our conclusions and to sharpen further our conceptual framework in preparation for applying our findings to contemporary circumstances.

Finally, because Christ fulfills the prophetic office, a deeper understanding of that office has direct implications for contemporary Christians. Romans 8:29 informs us that "those God foreknew he also predestined to be conformed to the likeness of his Son." If one dimension of the Son is his fulfillment of the prophetic office, it is logically inescapable that those being conformed to his likeness must also have a prophetic task. Our analysis of who a prophet is and what a prophet does will inform our understanding of what the church should be doing today. In the sixth chapter, we reflect upon the significance of the fact that the church is called upon to fulfill a prophetic role in the world today. What does this task look like in practical terms? How should the church undertake its responsibility in this regard? These are the questions that bring our study down from the realm of purely academic recreation to transformative personal and communal application. These are questions that must be answered and whose answers must be implemented if we are truly serious about following our Lord. Promoting the realization of the fruit of these questions in the life of the church is the goal of this book.

As I hope is clear by now, this book will not be surveying the biblical prophets ad seriatim as has been done sufficiently by any number of contemporary introductions to the prophetic books.[16] Rather, this book will be at the same time more comprehensive and more focused. It will be more comprehensive in that we will be examining the biblical prophetic phenomenon in its entirety from the written materials available to us. We will be developing an understanding of the prophets that is able to comprehend all of the data. Our study will also be more focused in that from its very beginning we have a clear goal for our efforts. We are not conducting this exercise for the purpose of producing an abstract and academically sterile volume having no apparent contemporary relevance. Instead, we will always be engaging the texts with a view toward applying what we find to our lives today.

---

16. See, for example, Freeman, *An Introduction to the Old Testament Prophets;* and John W. Miller, *Meet the Prophets: A Beginner's Guide to the Books of the Biblical Prophets—Their Meaning Then and Now* (New York: Paulist, 1987).

O N E

WHAT A PROPHET
IS NOT

When Sir Arthur Conan Doyle's great detective, Sherlock Holmes, sought to establish the facts of a case upon which he had focused his considerable mental powers, one of the precepts he applied was: "When you have eliminated the impossible, whatever remains, however improbable, must be the truth."[1] In a sense, we are now playing the role of detectives ourselves in seeking to establish the facts surrounding the mysterious characters called prophets, whom we find at work in the Old Testament. So we too may apply Holmes's precept to our own investigation. Is it possible to eliminate certain characteristics, behaviors, or other features of a prophet's life so that the remaining details leave us with a clearer understanding of the truth? The Bible enables us to answer this question affirmatively. Scripture itself informs us of certain things that are not allowed to play any part in the biblical

1. Consider, for example, Holmes's application of this precept in the mysterious case entitled "The Sign of the Four" in Sir Arthur Conan Doyle, *The Complete Sherlock Holmes* (Garden City, N.Y.: Doubleday, 1930), 111.

prophets' functions. When we have eliminated these from possible prophetic functions, what remains, however improbable, must be the truth. Two of the most significant passages that describe prohibited behaviors occur already in the fifth book of the Old Testament.

SCRIPTURAL PROHIBITIONS

Deuteronomy 13:1–5

In chapter 13 of Deuteronomy, we find Moses warning the people of Israel about the harmful influences that may seduce them away from fulfilling the demands of the covenant. The seduction he describes in the first five verses comes from a false prophet. While we are not given much specific information about what identifies this person as a false prophet, we *are* told that such a person encourages God's people to follow after other gods and worship them:

> If a prophet, or one who foretells by dreams, appears among you and announces to you a miraculous sign or wonder, and if the sign or wonder of which he has spoken takes place, and he says, "Let us follow other gods" (gods you have not known) "and let us worship them," you must not listen to the words of that prophet or dreamer. . . . That prophet or dreamer must be put to death, because he preached rebellion against the LORD your God.

One impossibility for a true biblical prophet, therefore, is that he would proclaim any message that promotes other gods or their worship. Conversely, one characteristic of a true prophet is that his message will encourage obedience and faithfulness to God. A true prophet calls people back to the requirements of the law and not to new theological paths. This is a difficult truth for some to accept these days when new and even radical theologies are in vogue and the ancient, historically forged and tested theological understanding of the church throughout the ages is regarded as dry, dusty, and hardly worthy of serious attention.

While it is not too surprising that false prophets would encourage a departure from the orthodox faith, another feature of this passage is a little more unexpected. For we are clearly told that the apostasy encouraged by a false prophet may be accompanied by a miraculous sign or wonder! This is disturbing for the simple reason that *true* prophets often pointed to signs as evidences of the truthfulness of their pronouncements.[2] When signs proceed from false prophets, it may be that they are the result of simple intelligence or happenstance. However, we learn from our passage that these signs of the false prophets may also be a means by which the Lord is testing his people to determine their loyalty: "The LORD your God is testing you to find out whether you love him with all your heart and with all your soul" (Deut. 13:3).[3] Since this is the case, we must also disallow fulfilled prophecy as *the* single defining characteristic of a true prophet. The signs or wonders the prophet performs are of secondary importance to the message they accompany. This no doubt explains Jesus' later frustration with those Jews who focused their attention so exclusively on miraculous signs (Matt. 12:39–42; John 4:48) while ignoring the revolutionary significance of his message.

2. Consider, for example, the sign provided by the unnamed "man of God" in 1 Kings 13:3, or Isaiah's sign for King Hezekiah in 2 Kings 19:29.

3. Gerhard von Rad, *Deuteronomy*, OTL (Philadelphia: Westminster, 1966), 97: "Did [the signs] come from Yahweh at all? Yes, they did; for behind such phenomena, too, there stands Yahweh, that is to say, he is using a deliberate divine method of teaching. In ways like this he devises a test of Israel's loyalty."

Today, we too must not allow ourselves to be similarly overawed by apparent signs of God's blessing in our churches, such as expansive facilities, growing congregations, flashy programs, and huge budgets, so that we fail to give proper attention to the messages we hear. God does not change. He still tests the loyalty of his people, and we are still responsible to check everything we hear over against established truth. Consider, for example, the Bereans, who had the privilege of listening to one whose credentials were impeccable—the apostle Paul. Yet, even though it was Paul who was speaking to them, Luke praises them for checking out Paul's message: "Now the Bereans were of more noble character than the Thessalonians, for they received the message with great eagerness *and examined the Scriptures every day to see if what Paul said was true*" (Acts 17:11). A person is not necessarily a prophet because he is able to announce a sign or wonder that comes to pass. If the message that person speaks calls people to faithful obedience to the God of the Scriptures, only then should the sign or wonder be acknowledged as legitimate.

Deuteronomy 18:9–13

In chapters 16–18 of Deuteronomy, Moses describes in detail the duties and responsibilities of those who hold special offices in the community of Israel. In Deuteronomy 16:18–20, he gives instructions regarding judges—how they are to be appointed and how they are to carry out their tasks. In Deuteronomy 17:8–13, Moses expands upon his instructions for judges to include those difficult cases that should be brought before the priests. In Deuteronomy 17:14–20, Moses talks about the time when the Israelites will demand a king. He explains the requirements and limitations associated with this office as well. After prescribing the appropriate provisions for the priests (Deut. 18:1–8), Moses proceeds to list what the people must not do when seeking a message from God. This fascinating passage (Deut. 18:9–13) is filled with information about the prophetic office in Israel and how it was to differ from those efforts at securing information from the deity that were practiced by the surrounding nations. Our understanding of the prophetic office must therefore exclude anything found in these verses. After eliminating these "impossibilities," we will be in a better position to deduce the true function of a biblical prophet from the remaining evidence. Let's consider these forbidden practices one at a time.

Child Sacrifice. It is not well understood what this practice entailed. It may have consisted of a simple, though gruesome sacrifice of one's own child as an expression of devotion to a god or, more probably, as a way to persuade the god to grant one's wishes. The specifics of how this was accomplished are lost to antiquity. Earlier in the book of Deuteronomy, we were informed that the nations inhabiting Canaan "burn their sons and daughters in the fire as sacrifices to their gods" (Deut. 12:31). Scripture informs us that one of these gods was Molech, the national god of the Ammonites, who is repeatedly mentioned in connection with this horrible practice.[4] Even Israelite kings such as Ahaz (2 Kings 16:2–3) and Manasseh (2 Kings 21:1–6) are guilty of sacrificing their children to this pagan deity. King Solomon too followed this god and built a high place for him on the Mount of Olives (1 Kings 11:5–7). The practice is also associated in some passages with divination; that is, a way of ascertaining desired information from the deity.

---

4. See Lev. 18:21; 20:2–5; 2 Kings 23:10; Isa. 57:9; Jer. 7:30–34; 32:35; Ezek. 16:20–22; 23:37–39. John Gray provides an excellent description of this Ammonite deity and its influence on Israelite culture in *IDB*, s.v. "Molech, Moloch," 3:422–23.

Ezekiel 20:30–31 contrasts this practice with inquiry of the true God, suggesting that the former involved inquiry of a pagan god. Leviticus 20:1–5 also forbids this procedure in verses that are immediately followed by a proscription against mediums and spiritists—again suggesting that this practice involved seeking information outside of the realm of accepted practice.

Now certainly there seems to be little fear these days of repeating this particular error of the past in our contemporary churches. Nevertheless, while the specific practice may be virtually extinct, the motivations and attitudes prompting it certainly aren't. We should note that the one who seeks to approach the deity by child sacrifice certainly cannot be faulted for a lack of devotion or zeal! It is hard to conceive of a greater expression of religious zeal than this. There is an important qualification for zeal, though, that we often ignore to our own harm. We read in Proverbs 19:2, "It is not good to have zeal *without knowledge,* nor to be hasty and miss the way." In our passage, the zeal of the sacrificer is completely uninformed by the word of God. The sacrificer illegitimately presumes the privilege of expressing his zeal and devotion in whatever way he chooses. Moreover, the ultimate goal of this practice seems to be to bend the will of the god to one's own will. In other words, the deity is subtly made to be a servant of his "follower."

We can certainly recognize this sort of topsy-turvy religiosity in our congregations today. We also demand to worship God in whatever way we choose. In fact, it almost seems that the more novel an idea is, the more we clamor to incorporate it into our worship services. It is no coincidence that preaching is becoming an increasingly smaller component of the liturgy. Demands for freedom to worship in whatever way we choose and a desire to be able to prompt God to perform our will (instead of asking him to help us perform his will) are still alive and well in the twenty-first century. Moses' words remind us that these motivations and attitudes are to play no role in the prophetic task.

Divination or Sorcery. These are probably umbrella terms that are used to denote a wide range of divinatory practices without specifying the particular means used in each case.[5] Moses follows this general heading with more specific examples.

Interpreting Omens. This involved a great variety of mechanical techniques for discerning the will of the gods, usually by the examination of the entrails of sacrificial animals (extispicy) or, more specifically, their livers (hepatoscopy; see Ezek. 21:21). Other items interpreted for their supposed divinatory content included heavenly bodies (i.e., astrology; see Isa. 47:13 and Dan. 2:2, 4), natural phenomena, births, arrows shot (Ezek. 21:21; 1 Sam. 20:18–42; 2 Kings 13:14–19), animals and birds, rods or sticks of wood (Hos. 4:12), and cultic images (Zech. 10:2).[6] John Walton explains that this practice reflected the belief that all of reality was an interlocking totality. This led to the conclusion that the events occurring at the same time as a particular phenomenon had a likelihood of occurring again when the same phenomenon recurred: "It was possible, and even likely, that history would repeat itself, but the purposes of the gods were indiscernible. The omen mentality gave the people some help in trying to figure out *when* history might repeat itself."[7]

---

5. Malcolm J. A. Horsnell, "קסם," in *NIDOTTE,* 3:945, states that this root signifies to "practice divination in general without indication of means."

6. Horsnell, "קסם," *NIDOTTE,* 3:946.

7. John Walton, *Ancient Israelite Literature in Its Cultural Context* (Chicago: Moody, 1992), 123. An instance of the king of Babylon "examining the liver" is found in Ezek. 21:21.

The fundamental problem with this practice of interpreting omens (apart from its specific prohibition in Scripture) is that it seeks to tell the future or uncover otherwise
hidden knowledge by means other than those which God
himself has appointed. Those who carry out this practice behave as though God were not necessary or were not inextricably involved in bringing to pass the future he has
ordained. It ignores the carefully crafted redemptive revelation that God provides in favor of practices tailored more to
the practitioner's desires or interests. It is an expression of
disobedience and faithlessness.

Even today we may find ourselves guilty of divination
when we seek to discover the future by means other than
those God has appointed and provided. Horoscopes, palm
readings, tea leaves, psychic hotlines, tarot cards, numerol-
ogy, scrying,[8] and many other avenues are offered to us as
alternative means for discovering our futures without reference to God. The fact is, there is no future worth considering apart from God. The true prophet is one whose insights
proceed from the only one who really knows what is to
come, and who gives all of life its ultimate meaning.

Witchcraft. This involves the practice of magic, including
the use of "spells, incantations, charms/amulets, and special
rituals to manipulate natural powers and to influence situations, people, and gods."[9] Exodus 7:11 links this practice to
the magicians and sorcerers in Egypt. Similarly, Daniel 2:2
links it to the magicians, sorcerers, and astrologers in Babylon. Malcolm Horsnell observes: "Magic sought to manipulate the divine world to satisfy human needs; it was more

---

8. This unfamiliar term describes the technique of gazing into a crystal ball,
black mirror, bowl of water, etc., in order to see into the future.

9. Horsnell, "כשׁף," *NIDOTTE*, 2:735–38.

human centered. . . . Ancient Israel's Yahwistic faith allowed
for divine revelation but not for manipulation of the divine
world."[10]

This illegitimate method of interacting with the natural
order is still in vogue in contemporary times in some seg-
ments of Western culture,[11] and even more so in other parts
of the world less influenced by Christianity. In this case too
instead of reliance upon the providential care of a loving
God who knows the end from the beginning, those who
practice witchcraft seek to manipulate people and events for
their own selfish ends. This practice even goes so far as to attempt to coerce the divine realm into the service of the practitioner. Once again, submission to the authority of God has
been replaced by efforts to get God to submit to human authority. A more subtle manifestation of this principle appears
when we co-opt religion as a handmaiden to our own success. There are those in the church whose main interest in
God and religion is how God and religion can serve their
own purposes. We need to reflect seriously on how we may
find in our own lives traces of this sin, which the Bible con-
demns. True biblical prophets, we may safely conclude, do
not use their office to attempt to manipulate God or others
for their own purposes.

Casting Spells. Literally, this translates as "one who knots
knots" (חֹבֵר חָבֶר, *hover haver*). Although the biblical and ancient Near Eastern evidence clearly indicates its connection

---

10. Horsnell, "קסם," *NIDOTTE*, 3:946.

11. On the basis of extensive research, B. A. Robinson, "How Many Wiccans Are
There in the U.S.?" (n.p. [cited 29 March 2002]. Online: http://www.religioustoler-
ance.org), estimates that there are "something on the order of 750,000 [Wiccans] in
the U.S. and perhaps 30,000 in Canada . . . making Wicca about the 7th largest or-
ganized religion in the United States." He also cites support for the disturbing conclusion that Wicca/neo-paganism is the fastest-growing religion in North America.

to sorcery,[12] the precise nature of this occult practice has been lost to history. Inasmuch as this practice is utilized to manipulate persons or events for one's own purposes, it poses the same fundamental problems as those practices already considered.

Spiritualism. This term refers to the practices of a medium or spiritist (שֹׁאֵל אוֹב וְיִדְּעֹנִי, *sho'el 'ov weyidde'oni*), or one who consults the dead (וְדֹרֵשׁ אֶל־הַמֵּתִים, *wedoresh 'el-hammetim*). These practices involve conjuring up and consulting the dead or ghosts on behalf of others. We find the witch of Endor engaging in this procedure for Saul in 1 Samuel 28:7–25. This practice is explicitly forbidden under penalty of death in Leviticus 19:31; 20:6, 27. Here, again, those who perform these forbidden practices are seeking to sidestep responsibility to God by endeavoring to gain access to hidden knowledge without any appeal to him.

This kind of godless spirituality has become very popular these days as well. There is a best-selling author and television host who offers to provide inquirers with information from those "on the other side." Those who represent themselves as mediums or, more popularly, as "channelers," are no longer viewed with disdain by the popular culture. Ouija boards and séances are used to attempt to communicate with the dead. Movies and books whose plots involve contact between human beings and the spirit world with no reference to God are smash hits. Even though the cultural trend is clearly toward acceptance of spiritists, we as Christians must shun these avenues in favor of the legitimate avenue God himself has appointed—the prophets.

All of these cultic and mantic practices are forbidden because they spring from a conception that is entirely at odds

12. See George J. Brooke, "חבר," in *NIDOTTE*, 2:16–18.

with biblical faith. They proceed on the fundamentally flawed notion that their practitioners are able somehow to obtain for themselves some measure of the divine power or knowledge, or are able to manipulate the deity in some way for their own ends. Moreover, these pursuits after wisdom and power properly belonging exclusively to the divine realm take place according to the desires and timing of the mantic practitioners rather than those of God. There are, of course, at the bottom of all this a terrible lack of faith in God's ability and providence and an arrogant assurance in one's own perspicacity. It's as though one were to say, "Thanks anyway, God, but I'd prefer to handle this situation myself." Such an attitude, manifested by such practices, has no place in the covenant community of God and his people. In the passages we have considered, God makes it clear that the prophetic task is characterized by different practices, motivations, and attitudes.

So we are not to regard the prophets as having some special ability to manipulate people, events, or even God for their own or their people's ends. Nor do they have the capability to pry into the divine counsel at times other than those that God himself chooses. How then should we regard them? What are their distinguishing characteristics that will enable us to identify them with certainty? We have made some progress in answering this question by eliminating some possible answers given by the Israelites themselves and their ancient Near Eastern neighbors. We are not limited, however, to ancient documents. Many modern scholars have wrestled with the question of *the* distinguishing feature of biblical prophets and have proposed some answers of their own. I have included these answers in this discussion of what a prophet is not because I believe that all of them are insufficient to account for all of the biblical data. They do provide helpful insights into and ingredients for the answer we're seeking, but not a complete recipe. Nevertheless, before we proceed to make some suggestions of our own, let's see what we can learn from the work of those who have gone before.

INADEQUATE PERSPECTIVES

Messengers

Many scholars have concluded that the essential function of a prophet—the function that explains all of his other actions—is that of a divine messenger.[13] Alexander Rofé argues that this perspective of the prophet's task is supported by the phraseology used to introduce the prophetic messages, namely, "Thus says the LORD": "In the world of the Bible this is the formula through which the messenger conveyed the words of his master, most specifically the words of his king (see for example Judges 11:15; 2 Kings 18:19, 29). The prophet is thus the messenger of a most mighty king."[14]

We should also note at this point that the messengers—of a human king or the divine king—deliver their messages

---

13. From the abundant examples that may be cited, consider Mary Evans, *Prophets of the Lord* (London: Paternoster, 1992), 17: "A prophet is someone who is called by God to perform a task or a set of tasks for him, and in particular to deliver a message from him"; David Noel Freedman, "Between God and Man: Prophets in Ancient Israel," in *Prophecy and Prophets*, ed. Yehoshua Gitay (Atlanta: Scholars, 1997), 61: "The prophet is the ambassador or messenger of God, and his/her sole duty is to deliver the message as given"; Robert G. Hamerton-Kelly, *The Divine Passion: Reflections on the Prophets* (Nashville: The Upper Room, 1988), 15: "Fundamentally, the prophet is a spokesperson for God"; E. W. Heaton, *The Old Testament Prophets* (Atlanta: John Knox, 1977), 29: "They [i.e., the prophets] were essentially *spokesmen*"; Gene Tucker, "Prophetic Speech," in James L. Mays and Paul J. Achtemeier, eds., *Interpreting the Prophets* (Philadelphia: Fortress, 1987), 27: "[The prophets'] basic vocation was to be as speakers who brought a communication from God"; and VanGemeren, *Interpreting the Prophetic Word*, 43: "The prophets were first and foremost speakers."

14. Alexander Rofé, *Introduction to the Prophetic Literature*, trans. Judith H. Seeligmann (Sheffield: Sheffield Academic Press, 1997), 61–62.

in the first person. This is evident, for example, in Genesis 32:3–5, where Jacob gives the content of the message to his designated messengers. These messengers are evidently supposed to deliver this message verbatim, as though it were proceeding from the mouth of its originator himself. Similarly, in 1 Kings 22:26–27, Ahab's messengers are given a message they are instructed to repeat verbatim in the presence of the designated recipients, prefaced by the phrase so familiar in the prophetic books, "Thus says the king." To these examples may be added those cited by Rofé above. A derivative point we should note is that the authority for the message is clearly that of the message sender.[15] Hence the need for the identification of the sender at the beginning of the delivery with the formula "Thus says X."

Because the behavior of the biblical prophets in their proclamation of the divine word so clearly parallels the behavior of other biblical messengers, it seems beyond dispute that delivery of divine messages was at the very least part of the prophet's responsibility. But was it the whole? Or is it legitimate to subsume every other biblically recorded behavior of a prophet under this one perspective? There *were*, after all, other functionaries within Israel and Judah who spoke for God. The priests, for example, had been assigned tasks that could also be viewed as delivering divine messages. These include blessing the people after the daily sacrifices (Lev. 9:22; Num. 6:23–27), declaring people clean when the appropriate conditions had been met (Lev. 13–14), addressing the troops before they entered into battle (Deut. 20:2–4), and, most importantly, instructing the people in the

---

15. Klaus Koch, *The Prophets,* vol. 1: *The Assyrian Period,* trans. Margaret Kohl (Philadelphia: Fortress, 1982), 22: "Thus says so-and-so is the phrase with which the ancient oriental kings and dignitaries legitimate themselves when sending verbal messages, or in their letters."

law and rendering verdicts in difficult legal cases (Deut. 17:8–13; 19:17; 21:5).

But the prophets had to contend not only with the words of the priests, but also with the official proclamations of kings. God had acquiesced to his people's demand for a king and had established an enduring royal line through David. It would be natural for the people to view this leader as God's vicegerent; that is, as the one whom God had designated to rule on his behalf. The words of the king, in addition to the fact that they proceeded from one having tremendous power to affect the life of every citizen, had authority derived from God himself.

The office of prophet, therefore, was not the only one that issued messages that the people would regard as having divine authority. How did the prophets interact with these other bearers of divine words? Were they at odds with the priests and kings, or did they work together with them for the good of the people of God? If we are eventually to arrive at a comprehensive understanding of the prophets that will influence our activity in the church today, this is not a question of purely historical interest. How one answers this question will obviously have a direct bearing on how one assesses the kind of interactivity that contemporary counterparts of the biblical prophets should have with other church functionaries today. Should that interaction be antagonistic or supportive? Contemporary authors have endorsed both positions.[16] But what help can we receive from those who have considered this question before us? As we will see, the ques-

---

16. Those promoting an antagonistic relationship include J. Elliot Corbett and Elizabeth S. Smith, *Becoming a Prophetic Community* (Atlanta: John Knox, 1980); Dan Allender, "Mimicking Our Disruptive Father and Our Diverse Older Brother," *Mars Hill Review* 5 (1996): 35–46; Patrick D. Miller Jr. "The Prophetic Critique of Kings," *Ex Auditu* 2 (1986): 82–95. For those who promote a more cooperative approach, see Alexander Rofé, *Introduction to the Prophetic Literature*, 75–77.

tion of the prophets' role with respect to the offices of priest and king has vexed biblical scholars for some time. Let us consider the prophets' interaction with each of these offices separately.

Antagonists or Supporters?

With Respect to Priests. The relationship between the prophets and the priests has produced considerable debate in the history of biblical studies. There is, of course, always a danger of caricaturing either side of the argument by summarizing what has been a rather protracted discussion in ways that favor our own position. Nevertheless, we may safely say that the essential question over which the disagreement arises is, "To what extent did the prophets participate in the formal religious rituals usually associated with the priests?"

There are many who argue on biblical grounds that the prophets not only did not participate in the formal rituals, but absolutely repudiated them.[17] One of the factors contributing to this conclusion is the view that religions evolve in the same way that biological entities are believed to have done. This view of the evolution of religions, which had its greatest influence in the late nineteenth and early twentieth centuries, holds that religion eventually evolves from the presumed dry, rigid, static, and confining formalities of ritualized worship into the enlightened, freeing, and contemporarily relevant worship of the Spirit.[18] The priests were regarded as representing the older type of worship, the prophets the later, more advanced stage. Hence, the

17. For a survey of those who hold such views, see Lloyd R. Bailey, "The Prophetic Critique of Israel's Cultic Order," *Faith and Mission* 6/2 (1989): 41–57.

18. The reader will surely notice the striking similarity between these two poles and the sides taken in the current debate over formal versus contemporary worship in the church.

prophets were regarded as antagonistic to the formal, cultic worship and its leaders, the priests. The scriptural passages appealed to in support of this view seem, at first, to provide overwhelming proof of its accuracy.

According to 1 Samuel 15:22, the Lord desires obedience rather than sacrifice. This is also the message of the prophets Hosea (6:6) and Jeremiah (7:22–23). The Lord seems to go further in Isaiah 1:11–13, where he uses very strong language indeed to express his dissatisfaction with his people's offerings: "The multitude of your sacrifices—what are they to me? . . . I have more than enough of burnt offerings. . . . I have no pleasure in the blood of bulls and lambs and goats. . . . Stop bringing meaningless offerings! Your incense is detestable to me."

This strong language continues in the prophecy of Amos, who declares in 5:21–25 that the Lord would give no regard even to the best and choicest offerings the Israelites could bring. Similarly, in Jeremiah 6:20 we read the prophet's message from the Lord that burnt offerings and sacrifices are not acceptable, but rather are displeasing to him.

Although such a collection of biblical passages seeming to support the antagonism of the prophets toward the priests appears formidable, this conclusion results from a failure to study such passages carefully. When we do so, it becomes obvious that what the prophets were condemning was not the sacrificial system itself, but rather the performance of these religious rituals without the proper attitude or mental posture toward God. In the words of the New Testament, such empty practices were performed by "lovers of pleasure . . . having a form of godliness but denying its power" (2 Tim. 3:4–5).

If the relationship between the prophets and the priests was not antagonistic, perhaps it was close—perhaps even very close. Some scholars have gone in this direction and concluded that far from representing an alternative religion separate from the formal religious practices associated with the priests, the prophets actually participated in such practices themselves. In academic shorthand, this view holds that the prophets were cultic functionaries.

Here too there are scriptural passages that seem to suggest that the prophets and the priests worked closely together. In many passages, the prophets and the priests are mentioned together.[19] In other passages, the prophets are associated with high places, such as Gibeah, Shiloh, and Mount Carmel—places of special religious significance usually associated with the priests (1 Sam. 9; 10:5–13; 1 Kings 11:29; 14:1–4; 2 Kings 4:22–25). To further complicate matters, we sometimes encounter priests and Levites prophesying. In 2 Chronicles 35:15, the descendants of Asaph are referred to as Levites. In 1 Chronicles 25:1–3, some of these descendants of Asaph—Levites—are set apart "for the ministry of prophesying." Similarly, in 2 Chronicles 34:30 the "priests and the Levites" were among those who went up to the temple of the Lord, but in the parallel passage in 2 Kings 23:2, it is "the priests and the prophets" who went up. Does this indicate that the functions of the priests and the prophets had become so compatible that the two offices had effectively merged into one?[20]

19. For example, Isa. 28:7; Jer. 4:9; 8:1, 10; 13:13; 14:18; 26:7, 16; 29:1; Lam. 4:13; Hos. 4:4–5; Mic. 3:11; Zeph. 3:3–4.

20. Rofé, *Introduction to the Prophetic Literature*, 76–77: "In the days of the monarchy the status of the prophets changed both socially and professionally. They became established as permanent functionaries of the Temple, side by side with the priests." Aubrey R. Johnson is perhaps the most significant proponent of the view that the prophets—at the very least the later ones—had been subsumed into the formal religious system and that their functions were performed within this system. His arguments, which draw on significantly more than we can deal with in our brief study, are set forth in his book *The Cultic Prophet in Ancient Israel*, 2d ed. (Cardiff: University of Wales Press, 1962).

Here, again, we need to consider some important details before drawing any conclusions. First, in the many passages in which priest and prophet are mentioned together we need to differentiate between true prophets and false ones. Many times the biblical prophets denounce corrupt priests and false prophets together (along with other groups), but this does not mean their responsibilities were the same. Second, unlike the priests, the prophets did not inherit their office, so it is unlikely that they were on the staff of the sanctuary. Third, God called some people to be prophets who were also of the priestly line,[21] but this does not mean that prophets and priests had the same functions any more than the fact that Paul the apostle made tents means that apostles and tentmakers have the same functions.

In conclusion, it is probably best to avoid both extremes when considering the prophets' role with respect to the priests. The prophets worked together with the priests in a complementary way for the spiritual development of the people of God, but they were free to criticize the priests when religious practices were becoming too formalized.

With Respect to Kings. The other office bearer with whom the prophets had to deal was the king. In this case as well there is some debate over how these two interacted. Again, we find two extremes—either the prophets were antagonistic to the kings, or the prophets collaborated with the kings.[22]

---

21. Consider, for example, Jeremiah (1:1) and Ezekiel (1:3).

22. Among those who highlight the antagonism of the prophets toward the kings are Simon DeVries, *Prophet Against Prophet: The Role of the Micaiah Narrative (1 Kings 22) in the Development of Early Prophetic Tradition* (Grand Rapids: Eerdmans, 1978), and Th. C. Vriezen, *An Outline of Old Testament Theology*, 2d ed. (Oxford: Blackwell, 1970). DeVries maintains (p. 148) that within Israel "the most central conflict was the constant polarity between the spiritual power of prophecy . . . and the political establishment."

Arguments for the former position usually include the fact that Israel's request for a king appears to have sprung from less than noble motives and seems to involve a rejection of the theocratic system that had characterized their community.[23] God himself maintains that by their request, the Israelites had rejected God as their king in favor of a human one (1 Sam. 8:7). It is also true that the prophets frequently pronounce judgments against kings. For example, Samuel rebukes Saul for disobeying the command of the Lord (1 Sam. 13:1–14). Later, Samuel again rebukes Saul for disobeying the Lord and pronounces the Lord's rejection of him as king (1 Sam. 15). Similarly, we find Nathan and Gad rebuking David (2 Sam. 12:1–14; 24:11–17); Hanani rebuking Asa (2 Chron. 16:7–9); and Hanani's son, Jehu, bringing God's word of condemnation to Baasha (1 Kings 16:1–4).[24]

The prophets cannot have been against kings per se, inasmuch as the book of Deuteronomy provided for one. Rather, it seems that the prophets were concerned to preserve the understanding that though there was a human king, he derived all of his authority from the true ruler of the people, God himself. That is, the prophets were striving to preserve the theocratic ideal—that the people were governed by God. This perspective has led some to label the prophets as "guardians of theocracy."[25] In other words, even though God had provided a king for Israel, the prophets labored to

---

23. 1 Sam. 8:5—"Appoint a king to lead us, such as all the other nations have."

24. To this abbreviated list we may add 1 Kings 14 (Ahijah and Jeroboam); 1 Kings 22 (Micaiah and Ahab); 2 Kings 1 (Elijah and Ahaziah); Isa. 7 (Isaiah and Ahaz); and Jer. 21–22 (Jeremiah and Zedekiah, Shallum, Jehoiakim, and Jehoiachin).

25. For example, Geerhardus Vos, *Biblical Theology: Old and New Testaments* (Grand Rapids: Eerdmans, 1948), 186, and Edward J. Young, *My Servants the Prophets* (Grand Rapids: Eerdmans, 1952), 82.

ensure that no one ever forgot that the human king was *not* to be "such as all the other nations have" (1 Sam. 8:5), but was to rule in a way that brought glory to God and not to himself.

Scripture is appealed to as well for the contrary view that the prophets had a much closer association with the monarchy than was afforded by periodic confrontation. In fact, some would say that the prophets had a semiformal position in the court as royal counselors.[26] This function is exemplified by Nathan's advice to David regarding the construction of the temple (2 Sam. 7:1–17) and Isaiah's advice to Hezekiah regarding the attack of Sennacherib (Isa. 36–39).[27] The prophets seem to have been particularly called upon to give advice to kings concerning the undertaking of military action. Samuel gives instructions to Saul regarding war with the Amalekites (1 Sam. 15:1–4). Elisha counsels Joram, king of Israel, and Jehoshaphat, king of Judah, regarding war with the Moabites (2 Kings 3:14–19). Moreover, we find the prophets announcing the establishment or fall of kings (e.g., 1 Sam. 10–11; 1 Kings 11:29–31; 14:1–11; 2 Kings 8:7–13).

All of this prophetic involvement in civil administration may lead to the erroneous conclusion that the prophets were essentially government servants, but this is not the case. As E. J. Young has summarized: "It would be a grave mistake . . . to assume that, because of the great interest of the prophets in the monarchy, they were themselves pri-

---

26. Rofé, *Introduction to the Prophetic Literature*, 75: "The prophet at the king's court has a well-defined role. If the individual occasionally needs help and guidance, how much more so does the king."

27. Other examples of the prophets providing counsel to kings abound. Consider, for example, Gad's counsel to David (1 Sam. 22:5); Nathan's counsel to David (1 Kings 1); Micaiah's counsel to Ahab (1 Kings 22); Elisha's counsel to Jehoash (2 Kings 13); and Isaiah's counsel to Ahaz (Isa. 7).

marily politicians. Their political activity is always sub-servient to a religious end. They did serve as counsellors, but they did so in order that the theocratic kingdom might prosper."[28]

It seems best to conclude, therefore, that just as was the case with the prophets' relationship with the priests, so it was with the kings. The prophets were not auxiliaries of the priests or the kings, but had their own distinct role to fulfill that at times brought them into conflict with one or both of these other officeholders. At other times, however, the prophets were able to work in concert with the priests and the kings for the physical and spiritual betterment of the people with whose care they had been entrusted.[29] Because the prophetic role is distinct from these other offices, identi-fying the primary prophetic function(s) as something sub-sidiary to that of the priests or the kings is not justified.

Mediators

Previously, we saw that at least part of the prophet's role consisted of carrying out the functions associated with an an-cient Near Eastern messenger. The prophet delivers mes-sages with the authority of the commissioning sender—in this case, God himself. However, to focus exclusively on this single direction of communication is to overlook another im-portant function of the prophet. The prophet also communi-cates to God on behalf of the people.[30] A prophet therefore carries out a mediatorial task, standing between God and his people, communicating from each party to the other.

---

28. Young, *My Servants the Prophets,* 82.

29. Cf. ibid.: "[The prophets'] work in one sense was to supplement that of the kings and the priests."

30. Freedman, "Between God and Man," 70: "In addition to the primary task of the prophet as messenger and spokesman for God, mention should also be made of another at least equally important role: intercessor on behalf of the people of God."

This responsibility to mediate the two-way communication between God and his people is a task usually associated with the priests. As we saw in the previous section, the roles of the prophets and priests are complementary and may overlap, while yet remaining distinct. The prophetic mediation on behalf of the people will be explored in greater detail in chapter 3, where we will discuss the specifics of what a prophet does. For now it is sufficient to note that the prophet speaks for the people as well as for God. For confirmation of this fact we need look only at "the most dramatic case of intercession,"[31] in which Moses intercedes with God concerning the sin of Israel involving the golden calf (Exod. 32).

While this perspective of a prophet's role adds substantially to our understanding and fills out the picture of this biblical figure to a great extent, *it is still inadequate* as an overall perspective of the prophetic function(s). For though we now accept that the prophet speaks for both God and his people, we have not yet investigated the content of that speech and the manner of its communication, whether the communication is limited to speech or includes other aspects or characteristics of the communicator. We have yet to find an overarching description of a prophet under which all of his tasks may be legitimately placed. So we continue on our journey of discovery by considering some further perspectives on the prophets provided for us by earlier explorers in this area.

Social Reformers

Related to the perspective discussed earlier where the prophets were viewed as antagonistic toward the priesthood and promoters of a more evolved and formally unencum-

---

31. Freedman, "Between God and Man," 70.

bered religion is the perspective that regards the primary prophetic function as social reform. This perspective focuses more on the prophets as forthtellers than as foretellers.[32] At least part of this shift away from regarding the prophets as foretellers is due to the rejection by critical scholars and liberal theologians of a legitimate predictive element in prophecy. At this point one may well ask how the prophets point us toward the coming of Christ if supernatural prediction is rejected. From the perspective of the prophets as social reformers, the answer is that they do so by pointing us toward the moral idealism that is to characterize human relations and that is exemplified by Christ. Thus the prophets are no longer considered as foretelling Christ, but encouraging the kind of life modeled by Christ.

This is, of course, a broad generalization for a noble endeavor to apply prophetic concerns to contemporary contexts. And there is absolutely no doubt that the prophets are concerned with human relations and social justice. There are numerous passages in which the prophets exhort God's people to give special care to the weaker members of society—that is, the four "withouts": (1) the poor, afflicted, or humbled (עָנִי, 'oni), who are without money or means of defending themselves against the more powerful; (2) the orphan (יָתוֹם, yatom), who is without parents to see to his welfare; (3) the widow (אַלְמָנָה, 'almanah), who is without a husband and provider in the patriarchal society; and (4) the

---

32. David Stacey, *Prophetic Drama in the Old Testament* (London: Epworth, 1990), 49, ties the origin of the phrase "forthtelling, not foretelling" to R. H. Charles (*A Critical and Exegetical Commentary on the Book of Daniel* [Oxford: Clarendon, 1929], xxvi) and explains this new understanding of the prophetic function to mean "that the prophet looked deeply into the affairs of his day and at the lessons of the past and to the nature of Yahweh; then he was able to proclaim, his fallible human nature doubtless charged by the Spirit, what the outcome of the contemporary situation would be."

sojourner or resident alien (גֵּר, *ger*), who is without the rights, protections, and privileges that society affords its citizens.[33] Indeed, the prophets repeatedly indict Israel/Judah for failing to carry out social justice within the covenant community.[34]

This stress on social justice is significant for a couple of extremely important reasons. First, the laws concerning interpersonal relations within the community were intended to reflect the righteousness of God. His compassion, kindness, mercy, and love for his people are supposed to be demonstrated by their compassion, kindness, mercy, and love for one another. When more powerful members of the community of God oppress weaker members for personal gain, they send exactly the wrong message to the Gentiles, to whom, after all, they were supposed to be "light." Second, and more specifically, Israel herself had been redeemed from slavery in Egypt—the place of her own oppression. To oppress other members of the community in the land to which she had been delivered was to demonstrate a callousness to human need exactly the opposite of what she had experienced. It was an exhibition of the worst kind of ingratitude and effectively undid the redemption that God had provided for *all* his people.

Social justice is, therefore, a legitimate emphasis in prophetic proclamation; but placing exclusive emphasis on this dimension of the prophetic task, as though it were the defining prophetic function, leads to contemporary

---

33. For emphasis on these groups of people with special needs see passages such as Is. 1:17; Jer. 7:5–7; 22:2–3; and Zech. 7:9–10. In their emphasis on special care for those members of the community in special need, the prophets are reiterating a concern found throughout the Scriptures; e.g., Exod. 22:21–27; Ps. 72:1–4, 12–14; Prov. 14:21, 31; 19:17; 22:9, 22–23; 23:10–11; 29:7.

34. See, for example, Isa. 1:23; 3:14–15; 10:1–2; Amos 2:6–7; 4:1; 8:4–6.

applications that are unbalanced and even harmful. One such application that gained momentum in the late nineteenth century was the social gospel movement.[35] Combined with an evolutionary view of the development of religion, this emphasis on social justice, fueled by the intolerable conditions of the Industrial Revolution, led to the subordination of every other interest of the church. Other sectors of the church reacted in fear to this overemphasis. No doubt this fear was exacerbated by the theological and political liberalism, as well as the ecumenism, usually associated with the social gospel movement. This negative reaction to the social gospel movement led many in the church to reject entirely the prophets' social concerns and to focus almost exclusively on the spiritual life. As a result, the evangelistic mandate was no longer viewed so broadly as to include the wider cultural mandate. After all, why polish the brass on a sinking ship? Like the Essenes of the Judean wilderness, this part of the church withdrew from involvement in society. Its salt was locked away in the cupboard—safe from contamination, but without influence.

Clearly, neither a focus on social justice to the exclusion of the gospel, nor a focus on a gospel so narrowly defined that it has no impact on the culture is desirable. Rather, the goal of the contemporary Christian should be a position somewhere in the middle, one that accepts the social responsibility enjoined by the prophets while not confusing this effort toward a harmonious and compassionate social order with the totality of the gospel. By itself, then, the view

35. For a description of this movement from the writings of its most notable proponent (Walter Rauschenbusch), see the convenient collection of Benson Y. Landis, *A Rauschenbusch Reader: The Kingdom of God and the Social Gospel* (New York: Harper & Brothers, 1957).

that seeks to subsume all of the prophetic tasks under the rubric of social reform is inadequate and ultimately mistaken.[36]

Until the day when a perfect society is realized, the prophetic task will certainly include calls for social reform. But the prophets were about much more than this. For example, regarding the prophets simply as agents for social reform does not necessitate a divine origin for their prophetic message. Indeed, Robert R. Wilson has suggested that the prophets were driven more by the need to maintain the backing of their support groups than by divine compulsion to utter the word of God.[37] Gary Herion has described the problems with this approach:

> In this view, the prophet's autonomy and individuality essentially have been stripped from him: his personal convictions, values and beliefs are either non-existent (which makes him a hypocrite) or more simply they are reflective of his particular (central or peripheral) group's interests (which makes him a spokesman). The prophet's genuine sense of any "good" transcending his social group's interests has been effectively denied.[38]

36. Lester L. Grabbe, *Priests, Prophets, Diviners, Sages: A Socio-Historical Study of Religious Specialists in Ancient Israel* (Valley Forge, Pa.: Trinity, 1995), 104: "The designation 'social critics' applies only to some of the prophets and then only in a general way to a few of their prophecies, while 'social reformer' seems hardly appropriate to any of them."

37. Robert R. Wilson, *Prophecy and Society in Ancient Israel* (Philadelphia: Fortress, 1980). He summarizes his views in his article "Interpreting Israel's Religion: An Anthropological Perspective on the Problem of False Prophecy," in *The Place Is Too Small for Us: The Israelite Prophets in Recent Scholarship*, ed. Robert P. Gordon (Winona Lake, Ind.: Eisenbrauns, 1995), 339–41.

38. Gary Herion, "The Impact of Modern and Social Science Assumptions on the Reconstruction of Israelite History," *JSOT* 34 (1986): 11.

While the prophet was surely influenced to some degree by the group supporting his ministry (an influence keenly felt by anyone in ministry today), we have seen that whatever else the prophets were, they were at least messengers of God and not of themselves or others. The testimony of Scripture is clear: "Above all, you must understand that no prophecy of Scripture came about by the prophet's own interpretation. For prophecy never had its origin in the will of man, but men spoke from God as they were carried along by the Holy Spirit" (2 Peter 1:20–21). We who wish to address prophetically the social ills of our own day should also ensure that the words we speak are rooted in Scripture and not in our "own interpretation" of what constitutes the ideal human society.

Ecstatics

Shifting our vantage point a bit from considerations of the defining characteristic of the prophets in terms of their function(s), we now turn to the view that the defining characteristic of the prophets is a particular psychophysical state called "ecstasy."[39] This psychophysical state is characterized by a detached or abnormal state of consciousness in which normal sensory input and mental function are interrupted and replaced by a consuming focus on revelatory experience.[40] The truth of the matter, however, is that this myste-

---

39. David L. Petersen, "Ecstasy and Role Enactment," in *The Place Is Too Small for Us*, 279–80, traces the development of the view of ecstasy as "constitutive for Israelite prophetic activity." Originating in the works of Bernhard Duhm (*Das Buch Jesaja* [Göttingen: Vandenhoeck & Ruprecht, 1982 reprint]) and Hermann Gunkel ("Die geheimen Erfahrungen der Propheten Israels," *Suchen der Zeit* 1 [1903]: 112–53), this view achieved its place of central importance in G. Hölscher's seminal work *Die Propheten: Untersuchungen zur Religionsgeschichte Israels* (Leipzig: J. Hinrichs, 1914).

40. Johannes Lindblom, *Prophecy in Ancient Israel* (Philadelphia: Fortress, 1962), 1–6, maintains that prophets are men of religion *(homines religiosi)*. He relates prophetic inspiration to poetic inspiration (which is associated with the Muses). When inspiration intensifies, it becomes ecstasy, which he defines as "an

rious state is extremely difficult to define for the simple reason that unless one personally experiences it, one is entirely dependent upon secondhand reports of what it entails. Such reports in Scripture are very rare and sketchy. Elias Andrews, describing ecstasy, candidly admits, "Appearing with great diversity universally, it defies rigid definition, and is better viewed collectively to cover conditions of trance, dream, vision, audition, rapture, frenzy, exultation, and related states ranging from entire absence of consciousness to complete or partial awareness."[41]

On the basis of biblical descriptions of at least some prophets, ecstasy is occasionally thought to include various bizarre behavioral phenomena.[42] While the scriptural evidence is slim, enough exists to raise at least the possibility of occasional peculiar prophetic behavior. In the book of Jeremiah, Shemaiah is quoted as directing Zephaniah the priest to "put any madman who acts like a prophet into the stocks and neck-irons" (29:26). In 2 Kings 9:11, one of Jehu's officers refers to a young prophet as "this madman." This comparison of prophetic behavior to insanity continues in Hosea 9:7, where the prophet/inspired man is labeled "a fool" or "a

---

abnormal state of consciousness in which one is so absorbed . . . that the normal stream of psychical life is more or less arrested. The bodily senses cease to function; one becomes impervious to impressions from without; consciousness is exalted above the ordinary level of daily experience; unconscious mental impressions and ideas come to the surface in the form of visions and auditions" (4–5). He further maintains that this unusual condition is also usually accompanied by abnormal psychophysical manifestations.

41. Elias Andrews, "Ecstasy," *IDB*, 2:22.

42. Cristiano Grottanelli, *Kings and Prophets: Monarchic Power, Inspired Leadership, and Sacred Text in Biblical Narrative* (Oxford: Oxford University Press, 1999), 92: "The verb 'to prophesy' does not mean precisely to 'make prophecies' but rather 'to behave like a prophet,' that is, like an ecstatic, or, better yet, like 'one possessed,' with connotations of madness."

maniac."[43] We should note, however, that Hosea attributes such a characterization of the prophets to Israel's sinfulness. This might indicate that the prophet did not actually behave like a madman, but only that his words were treated like a madman's by the unbelieving populace.

Perhaps also indicating abnormal behavior is Jeremiah 23:9, where Jeremiah claims to have become "like a drunken man" or "a man overcome by wine" because of the Lord and his holy words. On the other hand, Jeremiah's words could be explained simply as his reaction to the dark content of the message he had received rather than a physical manifestation exhibited during its reception. Today we might express a similar reaction with the idiom "going weak in the knees."

Nevertheless, some passages appear unambiguously to indicate unusual behavior associated with prophesying. In 1 Samuel 10:5–6, Saul is told that he would meet a company of prophets and that he too would prophesy and "be changed into a different person."[44] In 1 Samuel 19:20–24, Saul's detachments of soldiers sent to capture David are incapacitated once they begin to prophesy. When Saul himself goes to David, he too is incapacitated by prophecy. Additionally, we are told that he stripped off his robe and "lay that way all day and night."

There seems to be little doubt that abnormal behavior occasionally accompanied prophecy, but certainly not always. How are we to explain this inconsistency? Around this question another great debate has raged. In general, those who hold to an evolutionary view of the development of Israelite religion explain the inconsistent manifestation of ecstasy-induced be-

---

43. The words "madman" (Jer. 29:26; 2 Kings 9:11) and "maniac" (Hos. 9:7) both translate the same Hebrew word (מְשֻׁגָּע, *meshugga'*), whose root (שׁגע) means "raving, crazy" (Chou-Wee Pan, "שׁגע," *NIDOTTE*, 4:46).

44. Literally, "another man" (אִישׁ אַחֵר).

havior by making a distinction between the early (also called
nonwriting or precanonical) and the later (also called writing
or canonical) prophets.[45] The early prophets are viewed as ec-
statics or "prophets of the Spirit," while the later prophets, or
"prophets of the word," are not.[46]

Such distinctions, however, go far beyond what the data
warrant. Hobart Freeman has nicely summarized the only
legitimate conclusion from the biblical evidence:

> From all this evidence it is quite apparent that the
> distinction between the precanonical prophets and
> the canonical prophets in which the former are said
> to be ecstatic $n^e bh\hat{\imath}$'$\hat{\imath}m$ who were Spirit-possessed,
> and the latter refined recipients of the word of the
> Lord, is both arbitrary and artificial. The true
> prophets of Israel, whether precanonical or canonical,
> possessed *both* the *word* and the *Spirit* of the Lord.[47]

Other scholars have gone in the other direction, denying
the existence of anything like the frenzied ecstatic behavior
exhibited by the pagan prophets. Freeman basically rede-
fines ecstasy as the "revelatory, prophetic state" that over-
takes the prophet during times of reception of divine
revelation. Abnormal behavior on the part of the prophets is
explained as nothing more than the response one would expect to a supernatural communication. The strange behavior
involved with the symbolic acts performed by the prophets
is certainly abnormal, but hardly the result of an ecstatic

---

45. See, e.g., R. B. Y. Scott, *The Relevance of the Prophets* (New York: Macmillan,
1944), 45–46.

46. This distinction between Spirit-prophecy and word-prophecy was introduced by Sigmund Mowinckel, "The Spirit and the Word in Pre-exilic Reform
Prophets," *JBL* 53 (1934): 199–227.

47. Freeman, *Introduction to the Old Testament Prophets*, 58.

state. Thus Freeman concludes, "The Scriptures do not deny the reality of some form of an ecstatic experience to the Hebrew prophets, but describe it as a *divinely induced revelatory condition* of a more or less restrained nature which was not on a continuum with pagan prophetism."[48]

Underlying all of these arguments about ecstasy and whether or how it was manifested among the biblical prophets is an uncomfortable reality: no one knows exactly what ecstasy is or what it involves. Its amorphous character renders it capable of being defined and described in whatever way suits the need of the argument. Ecstasy does not appear to be a necessary component of prophecy inasmuch as it is very often not mentioned.[49] It is not clear, therefore, that pursuing this perspective will add much, if anything, to our goal of translating the prophetic function(s) into contemporary Christian experience. Moreover, ecstasy cannot be the sine qua non of prophecy, because it pertains primarily to the individual prophetic experience and not to the prophet's interaction with others.[50] As Johannes Lindblom correctly notes, "That which distinguishes a prophet from other *homines religiosi* is that he never keeps his experiences to himself; he always feels compelled to announce to others what he has seen and heard."[51] The experience was not for the prophet's private enjoyment. Focusing on ecstasy as something to be emulated today will not only set before us a goal with no clear definition (and thus impossible to

48. Ibid., 62.

49. This is a fact pointed out with great ability by Abraham Heschel, *The Prophets* (New York: Harper & Row, 1962), 352–53.

50. But cf. the disagreement of Hölscher, cited by Petersen, "Ecstasy and Role Enactment," 280, who contends "ecstatic behavior was part of the prophet's public performance."

51. Lindblom, *Prophecy in Ancient Israel*, 1–2. Lindblom also maintains (p. 310), contrary to Hölscher, that far from being a central feature of prophetic life, ecstasy was "an accessory and accidental phenomenon."

achieve with any certainty), but also make private an office with primarily public responsibilities. While allowing that ecstasy, however understood, may occur because of or during the reception of divine revelation, we reject further speculation on this issue as ultimately unhelpful for our purposes.

CONCLUSION

After considering all of the evidence of a negative sort, we may conclude that there are several very specific things a prophet is not. Other suggestions for the distinguishing characteristic of a prophet, while yielding helpful components of the comprehensive picture, are not comprehensive in themselves. The following list summarizes our findings:

1. A true prophet does not lead people away from God.
2. A true prophet is not identified exclusively by his ability to perform a sign or wonder.
3. A true prophet does not seek to manipulate people, events, or God for his own purposes.
4. A true prophet does not perform his task by going around God.
5. A true prophet is more than a messenger.
6. A true prophet is not fundamentally characterized by his disposition toward priests or kings.
7. A true prophet is more than a mediator.
8. A true prophet is more than a social reformer.
9. A true prophet is not fundamentally characterized by ecstasy.

All of the descriptions of a biblical prophet that we have considered so far are lacking in some respect, and this might lead us to a degree of pessimism regarding the possible success of our study. After a somewhat frustrating investigation in which we hit one foul ball after another out of the theological park, we may well be ready to agree with that great contemporary philosopher, Calvin (no, not John Calvin, but the boy of that name in the Calvin and Hobbes comic strip), who exclaimed in exasperation, "The harder I work, the behinder I get!" It is not true, however, that we have not made any progress at all in our efforts at understanding biblical prophets. By heeding Holmes's advice and first considering all of the things a prophet is *not*, we have already safeguarded ourselves against many potential wrong turns and dead ends. Also, by eliminating the impossible, we have considerably narrowed the field on what *is* possible. Our field of vision will be further focused in the next chapter by the optometric power of Scripture as we consider the positive evidence for what a prophet *is*.

FOR FURTHER REFLECTION

1. What are some contemporary ways by which people seek to find out the future instead of studying what God has revealed in the Scriptures? What are the possible motivations for doing this?
2. What is the danger of focusing primarily on religious enthusiasm in our efforts at approaching God? What is necessary to safeguard us from the errors to which this enthusiasm might lead?
3. Reflect on how you might have used your faith or place in the church to attempt to manipulate people, events, or even God.
4. Describe the problems associated with seeing the prophetic task as primarily engaging social concerns. Describe the errors associated with regarding the prophetic task as essentially oblivious to social concerns.
5. What do you understand the essential function of a prophet to be?

T W O

WHAT A PROPHET IS

W e may be inclined to frame our discussion of what a prophet *is* in terms of what a prophet *does,* but these are really two entirely different matters that must be considered separately. The fundamental idea behind the prophetic office (what a prophet is) will find expression in every individual act the prophet performs (what a prophet does). Others may occasionally perform one or more of those acts—we have already seen that the responsibilities of the priests and kings overlapped those of the prophets—but we must understand the essence of the prophetic office before we can understand its concrete manifestations. Perhaps an example may help to clarify the distinction.

Suppose you walked past the open door of an office and, looking in, saw a person talking on the phone. Here is a specific activity with which you no doubt have great familiarity, but which nonetheless tells you very little about the person actually *doing* the activity. What is the essential perspective from which we are to understand the performance of this specific task by this specific person? Is this person a receptionist, whose primary duties include answering the phone? Is this person a pastor, dispensing advice over the phone to a parishioner? Is this person a business executive, teleconferencing with a colleague? Or perhaps this person just stopped by to use the office phone to call a tow truck for his disabled car. How we view the main function or functions of the person using the phone colors how we view the performance of this particular task (and every other task). So before we begin to describe the specific tasks the prophets perform in carrying out the responsibilities of their office, we need to develop a basic perspective from which we may view their activities in the appropriate light. Only then will we be able to understand them correctly.

In order to accomplish this purpose, we will pursue several different avenues of inquiry. First, we will survey the Hebrew words used in the Bible to describe this unique biblical figure in order to determine what help they may give us toward understanding his primary function. Second, we will note and consider more deeply the one feature about prophets that everyone agrees constitutes an important initial element of their office—their call. Third, by examining some pivotal scriptural passages that speak in a general way about the prophetic office, we will ensure that whatever specific perspective we arrive at will at least fit well within the general guidelines laid out in Scripture. Finally, we will bring all of these data together into a coherent conclusion, which will inform the rest of our study and enable us to understand and appreciate more fully the specific prophetic tasks that we will investigate in the next chapter.

TERMINOLOGY

First, let's take a look at the Hebrew words used to denote a prophet and see what contribution they may make toward our understanding of this enigmatic biblical figure.

The most common word for prophet in the Hebrew

Bible is *navi'* (נָבִיא). The meaning of this word is difficult to determine from a consideration of the Hebrew language alone because it is used in the Bible only to refer to the office we are presently considering.[1] Some commentators find the basic meaning of this word to be active; that is, a prophet is one who "calls out" or "speaks forth" the word of God.[2] Support for this view is adduced from the lexicon of William Gesenius,[3] who argues that the Hebrew verb *nava'* (from which the noun *navi'* is derived) is a "softened" form of the verb *nava'* (by "softened" he is referring to the change in the last consonant from *ayin* to *aleph*), which means "to flow, boil up, bubble forth." The Hebrew word for "prophet" is therefore understood to mean one from whom words "bubble forth" under divine inspiration in a state of religious agitation usually referred to as ecstasy. This interpretation of the word, which appears to be driven more by a prior conviction that the prophets were characterized by "ecstasy" than by any direct connotation of the word itself,[4] is further disadvantaged by the fact that the change in final consonant

---

1. Lester L. Grabbe, *Priests, Prophets, Diviners, Sages,* 108: "The origin of *nāvî'* . . . 'prophecy,' is not agreed. . . . There is no reason not to think of the root as a native Hebrew word, and any attempt to see it as a foreign borrowing has little to commend it. On the other hand, the word is not transparent and has no uses outside the prophetic context; therefore, to come up with a precise definition is difficult."

2. Freeman, *Introduction to the Old Testament Prophets,* 37–40; and John F. A. Sawyer, *Prophecy and Biblical Prophets* (Oxford: Oxford University Press, 1993), 1.

3. William Gesenius, *A Hebrew and English Lexicon of the Old Testament,* trans. Edward Robinson, 3d ed. (Boston: Crocker & Brewster, 1849), 525.

4. Gesenius, *Hebrew and English Lexicon,* 638–39. Cf. Grabbe, *Priests, Prophets, Diviners, Sages,* 108: "The term 'ecstatic behavior' has been seen as the basic connotation. This, however, is based on only a few passages, such as 1 Samuel 10:10–11; 19:20–24; and 1 Kings 18:26–29. Many other passages give no hint that a particular sort of behavior is implied beyond that associated with prophecy in general. The word seems to cover the entire variety of activity associated with prophecy including, but not limited to, ecstatic behavior."

this interpretation requires is extremely rare; "softening" does not regularly take place in the language.

We are on much firmer ground when we seek to determine the meaning of this word by examining cognate words in other Semitic languages. In the Akkadian language, one of the meanings of the verb *nabu* is "to decree, to proclaim, to command, to make known."[5] This would tend to add support to the view that we are to understand the prophet as one who proclaims the word of God. However, the more common meaning of the verb in Akkadian is "to name, give a name."[6] By extension—and this is a use that also occurs in English—this "naming" can imply appointing (or calling) a person to office. For example, in Akkadian texts *nabu* can refer to *appointing* people to "shepherdship" or "kingship."[7] Thus the cognate verb in Hebrew is usually understood in a passive sense; that is, one who is called or appointed by God.[8] This passive sense is further supported by a very regular feature of Semitic languages in which the *a–i* vowel pattern indicates a passive sense; that is, the action of the verb is done to the subject of the verb.[9] It seems extremely likely,

5. *CAD*, 11:37–38.

6. *CAD*, 11:33–35.

7. *CAD*, 11:35–37.

8. William F. Albright, *From the Stone Age to Christianity* (Garden City, N.Y.: Doubleday, 1957), 303: "One who is called [by God], one who has a vocation [from God]." See also Klaus Koch, *The Prophets*, 1:16: *navi'* "probably means literally 'entrusted with a message.'" For further discussion on this issue, see P. A. Verhoef, "Prophecy," *NIDOTTE*, 4:1067–78 (and especially pp. 1067–68).

9. Sabatino Moscati, ed., *An Introduction to the Comparative Grammar of the Semitic Languages: Phonology and Morphology* (Wiesbaden: Otto Harrassowitz, 1980), 146 (§16.69); and Bruce K. Waltke and M. O'Connor, *An Introduction to Biblical Hebrew Syntax* (Winona Lake, Ind.: Eisenbrauns, 1990), 88 (§5.3c), who note that the *qatil* pattern "is used for professional terms, some passive in sense." Waltke and O'Connor provide the following examples from Hebrew: אָסִיר (prisoner = one bound); מָשִׁיחַ (anointed one); and פָּלִיט (refugee = one given refuge). Nevertheless, they list נָבִיא under the "stative or active" use of this pattern.

therefore, that the best understanding of the sense of the noun is passive "one who is called."

Many passages of Scripture also refer to a prophet as a *ro'eh* (רֹאֶה) or a *hozeh* (חֹזֶה).[10] Both of these words have the basic meaning "to see."[11] That they are used to indicate prophets is beyond dispute. In 1 Samuel 9:9, for example, we are told in a parenthetical remark: "Formerly in Israel, if a man went to inquire of God, he would say, 'Come, let us go to the seer [*ro'eh*],' because the prophet [*navi'*] of today used to be called a seer." Clearly, then, the difference between the words *ro'eh* and *navi'* is merely chronological. These words simply refer to the same thing during different periods of time.

The other word for prophet, *hozeh*, is also unmistakably used to indicate the same thing as *navi'*. In 2 Samuel 24:11, the terms are used interchangeably to refer to the prophet Gad: "Before David got up the next morning, the word of the LORD had come to Gad the prophet [*navi'*], David's seer [*hozeh*]."

It is tempting to speculate about what it is that the prophet or seer "sees." Some reasonably propose that "seeing" (*ro'eh* and *hozeh*) refers to "the method of receiving the divine communication."[12] While we have not yet established that the revelation that is "seen" is necessarily of divine origin, that such is the case seems obvious from the fact that

10. *Ro'eh*: 1 Sam. 9:9, 11, 18, 19; 1 Chron. 9:22; 26:28; 29:29; Isa. 30:10; *hozeh*: 2 Sam. 24:11; 2 Kings 17:13; 1 Chron. 21:9; 25:5; 29:29; 2 Chron. 9:29; 12:15; 19:2; 29:25, 30; 33:18, 19; 35:15.

11. Jackie A. Naudé, "ראה," *NIDOTTE*, 3:1007–15; and idem, "חזה," *NIDOTTE*, 2:56–61.

12. Freeman, *Introduction to the Old Testament Prophets*, 40. See also Naudé, "ראה," *NIDOTTE*, 3:1007: "The verb is also used in the sense of becoming psychologically visionary conscious, seeing in a vision, receiving a revelation"; and "חזה," *NIDOTTE*, 2:58: "The verb [*hzh*] relates to the revelatory vision granted by God to chosen messengers, i.e., the prophets."

the two words are often used in conjunction with a prophet communicating a message to God's people that must of necessity have been received by some mysterious, divinely initiated manner beforehand. For example, in 2 Kings 17:13 we read, "The LORD warned Israel and Judah through all his prophets and seers." Although the exact methodology involved in delivering this warning to the prophets and seers is not discussed at all, it is clear that it came from the Lord. In Isaiah 30:10–11, we learn that the visions "seen" by these seers/prophets did, in fact, proceed from "the Holy One of Israel" and that their content was communicated to God's people (even though it was often unwelcome): "They say to the seers, 'See no more visions!' and to the prophets, 'Give us no more visions of what is right! Tell us pleasant things, prophesy illusions. Leave this way, get off this path, and stop confronting us with the Holy One of Israel!'" Thus it appears as though the people were well aware that the content of the prophetic messages came, at least at times, by way of visions provided to the prophets by God himself.

Our cursory review of the biblical terminology used in connection with the prophets has yielded the beginnings of a basic understanding of the perspective by which we should regard the biblical prophets and their behavior: they have been called and they "see" things not usually perceived by others. While the precise nature of the "seeing" seems impenetrable to our probing, we are able to make some headway with respect to the initial qualification for the prophetic job: the divine call.

THE PROPHETIC CALL

Whatever we are ultimately to understand about the tasks of the prophets, we must at least acknowledge that they have been called to do them.[13] While even in this area we must acknowledge that much mystery exists, we are not entirely ignorant of the details of these prophetic calls. In fact, the biblical narratives that describe them have a remarkable consistency in their details that enables us to recognize when we have stumbled upon one in our reading. These details form a pattern that contains the following elements:[14]

1. Divine confrontation
2. Introductory word
3. Commission
4. Objection from the prophet
5. Reassurance from God
6. Some sign from God confirming his intent

The divine confrontation is simply the preliminary contact God initiates with the future prophet whom he has decided to call. In the call of Moses,[15] for example, in Exodus 3:1–3, this preliminary contact consists of the angel of the Lord appearing to Moses "in flames of fire from within a bush." This definitely gets Moses' attention! He turns aside

---

13. Frank H. Seilhamer, *Prophets and Prophecy: Seven Key Messengers* (Philadelphia: Fortress, 1977), 2: "If there is one characteristic that was common to all biblical prophets it was their absolute assurance that God had called them personally into his service"; Evans, *Prophets of the Lord,* 30: "One of the most significant areas in a prophet's experience was his conviction of being called by God to the task that he had undertaken"; and Lindblom, *Prophecy in Ancient Israel,* 182: "In Israel the certainty of being called by Yahweh was one of the most characteristic features of the prophetic consciousness."

14. See, for example, N. Habel, "The Form and Significance of the Call Narratives," *ZAW* 77 (1965): 297–323.

15. Although many other prophets could be chosen to illustrate the call, Moses has been selected because "for Jews and Christians alike, Moses counts as being the prototype of a prophet" (Koch, *The Prophets,* 1:16).

to see "this strange sight" and is thereby placed in a physical and psychological position to hear the divine words that will be addressed to him.

The introductory word that follows this divine confrontation usually provides some further explanatory or descriptive details regarding the identity of the speaker and may also provide some background for the formal commissioning that will follow. In Moses' case (Exod. 3:4–9), God calls to Moses and, after receiving his response, identifies himself as the God of his fathers, the covenant God of Abraham, Isaac, and Jacob. He then proceeds to explain the reason for his appearance to Moses: his intention to deliver his covenant people from their mistreatment at the hands of the Egyptians.

This introductory word is followed by the formal commissioning of the prophet, which constitutes the essence of the prophetic appointment. In this component of the divine call, the prophet is formally charged by God to carry out a specific task, usually involving the delivery of a specific message. This formal commissioning very often includes some form of the verbs "go" and "send." In Exodus 3:10, both of these verbs are found in the commissioning of Moses: "So now, *go*, I am *sending* you to Pharaoh to bring my people the Israelites out of Egypt."

At this point in the prophet's call, we usually read about some sort of objection the prophet feebly, but understandably, offers as a response to the weighty responsibility he is being called to shoulder. The prophet often claims to feel personally inadequate to carry out the task and may subtly, though always ineffectively, request a divine reconsideration. We find Moses expressing such an objection in Exodus 3:11.

These prophetic objections are met with divine reassurance that God, in fact, knows what he is doing and is certainly capable of making the prophet effective. The heavenly encouragement usually consists of a pledge by God that he will be with the prophet every step of the way his obedience to the divine call takes him. Thus, in these reassurances, it is very common to find the words "Do not fear" or "I will be with you." In the first part of Exodus 3:12, this is precisely what God says to Moses.

As a further reassurance and guarantee to the prophet that he would effectively use his prophet to carry out his will, God usually follows up his verbal encouragement with a visible sign—something that either takes place at that time or will take place in the future. In Moses' call, the sign given by God is the pledge that after their deliverance, God's people will worship him "on this mountain" (Exod. 3:12).

These are the ingredients that are usually found in a prophetic call. Although not all of them are found in every prophetic call narrative, they are usually present in sufficient number to leave us in no doubt about what is happening.

Even though it may appear from this analysis that the prophetic call is well understood, a great deal of mystery remains.[16] How the communication from God impinges itself upon the consciousness of the prophet is not at all clear. We know it happens, but we, looking in at the prophet's experience from outside, don't know how it happens. We know the essentials of its content, but relatively little of its methodology. Nevertheless, the prophets themselves had absolutely no doubt about what had happened to them. Their calls had a profound impact on their lives. Having received such a divine experience, the prophets were impelled forward into

16. Lindblom, *Prophecy in Ancient Israel,* 6: "The call often takes [the prophet] by surprise. . . . The call has the character of a supernatural experience. It exceeds all human reason. It is often accompanied by physical and psychical phenomena. The call is frequently met with fear and trembling; but it is always regarded as an act of divine grace."

their ministries, often reluctantly, but with confidence that God had chosen them for a specific task and would see them through to its completion.[17]

The prophet has indeed been called by God for some purpose. However, we need to progress significantly further in our investigation before we may safely add any details to our understanding of *what,* specifically, the called person is called to do or *how* the called person carried out his appointed task. Here again we are utterly dependent upon the testimony of Scripture itself for any insight into these aspects of the office of our divine appointees.

SCRIPTURAL GUIDELINES

While many biblical passages and even entire biblical books depict the specific behaviors of the prophets, a few passages lay out for us some general principles that we need to understand before we will be able to establish any comprehensive picture of the prophetic office.

Exodus 4:10–16

This passage describes the well-known episode of Moses' objection to his prophetic calling to go to Pharaoh to bring the Israelites out of Egypt (3:10). The task God had called Moses to perform would require him to do a lot of public speaking. Moses, like so many of us, expresses grave doubt about his ability in this area: "O Lord, I have never been eloquent, neither in the past nor since you have spoken to your servant. I am slow of speech and tongue" (4:10). To this objection God responds with words that give us some

---

17. Lindblom, *Prophecy in Ancient Israel,* 182: "[The prophetic call] certainly was an impelling force in the lives of the prophets and at the same time a source of confidence and fortitude."

insight into his communication with Moses, as well as with future prophets: "I will help you speak and will teach you what to say" (4:12).

Nevertheless, again sounding surprisingly like some modern Christians, Moses requests that God choose someone else to do this difficult work (4:13). At this point God graciously provides for Moses, and for us, an explanation of at least part of the dynamics of the relationship between God and his prophets: "You shall speak to [Aaron] and put words in his mouth; I will help both of you speak and will teach you what to do. He will speak to the people for you, and it will be as if he were your mouth and as if you were God to him" (4:15–16). We learn from this passage that God puts his words into the mouth of the prophet and enables him to speak *and to act* as God desires. By telling Aaron what to say, by putting words in his mouth, Moses would be doing the same thing that God does for his prophets. In this way, Moses would be like God to Aaron. We should also note that this passage states that God will also teach Moses and Aaron "what to do." The aspect of the prophetic office that involves doing is often neglected by contemporary exegetes. This area of the prophetic task, though unelaborated upon in this passage, we must keep in mind as we formulate our description of the role of the prophet.

Exodus 6:28–7:5

This passage expands further upon the incident described above. The relationship that God has established between Moses and Aaron, in which Aaron speaks for Moses, is like that between God and a prophet: "Then the LORD said to Moses, 'See, I have made you like God to Pharaoh, and your brother Aaron will be your prophet. You are to say everything I command you, and your brother Aaron is to tell Pharaoh to let the Israelites go out of his country'" (7:1–2).

Here again we must remember that this passage does not present us with a comprehensive list of responsibilities associated with the prophetic office, but does give us one indisputable one: the prophet speaks the words of God. Another interesting detail appears in this passage as well. Moses and Aaron are commanded to speak to Pharaoh. This indicates that the prophetic message is not restricted to the people of God. The prophets could also be directed to deliver their messages to those outside of the covenant community.

Numbers 12:6–8

These verses are part of God's response to Miriam's and Aaron's opposition to Moses. In his response to their antagonism toward his leader, God describes the special relationship Moses enjoyed with him, a relationship that was unlike that experienced by any other prophet. In the course of God's elucidation of the unique aspects of his communication with Moses, he gives us some information about how he usually communicates with prophets. God says that he communicates with them "in visions" and "in dreams." This is unlike the way he speaks to Moses; that is, "clearly and not in riddles": "When a prophet of the LORD is among you, I reveal myself to him in visions, I speak to him in dreams. But this is not true of my servant Moses; he is faithful in all my house. With him I speak face to face, clearly and not in riddles; he sees the form of the LORD" (12:6–8).

A couple very important inferences may be drawn from these verses. First, God both reveals and conceals through the prophets. He reveals in that he gives them a revelation to deliver; he conceals in that the message is not communicated "clearly." Rather, it is unclear and may even be a riddle. The idea that God may communicate in a manner that in some ways obscures or hides his meaning may initially disturb us, but there are many indications in Scripture that he does precisely this. There is a familiar prophetic refrain regarding people who are "ever hearing, but never understanding."[18] This implies that comprehension of the meaning of the prophetic message may require further mental effort than just hearing. Jesus informs his disciples that his parables accomplish the same purpose of obscuring "the knowledge of the secrets of heaven" from some, but revealing those secrets to those who have ears to hear (Luke 8:9–10). Clearly the eyes (and ears) of faith are necessary for understanding prophetic communication, but even the faithful need to listen carefully and think about what they have heard.

A second conclusion we may draw from this passage is simply that because the prophetic messages are unclear and perhaps even in riddles, we must be very careful in the way we read and understand them. At an absolute minimum, we must say that there are at least some prophecies that must not be taken literally. Indeed, to take them literally would be to ignore God's own words, which inform us that they are unclear and enigmatic. A rigid literalism, therefore, in interpreting the prophets is contrary to Scripture's own teaching. This is an important guideline for us to remember in our efforts to apply the prophetic message to our contemporary situation.

Deuteronomy 18:14–22

We considered Deuteronomy 18:9–13 in chapter 1. It contained prohibitions against seeking God in the way Israel's pagan neighbors consulted their gods. The practices of these other nations were characterized by a desire to use or manipulate people, events, or even their gods to accomplish

---

18. See, for example, Isa. 6:9–10; 42:20; and Jer. 5:21; as well as Deut. 32:28 and Matt. 13:10–15.

their own desires. In contrast to such human-centered approaches, the correct way of receiving information from God is described in the second part of this passage—verses 14–22. In these verses we are told that God puts his words in the mouth of his prophets, in his own time and for his own purposes. Those who hear the divine message have a responsibility to respond appropriately. Moses warns that the people would have to give an account of themselves to God if they failed to respond to the divine message communicated to them by the prophets. However, even if such a responsibility is obediently accepted, we are still faced with the obvious question of how to tell whether the words heard are truly from God. The Israelites were confronted, as we are today, with many pious-sounding charismatic speakers who professed to be speaking the word of God. How could they (and we) tell who was legitimate and who was merely using the trappings of religion for personal enrichment?

Moses addresses this problem by stipulating that a prophet does not speak for the Lord if what he says does not come to pass: "You may say to yourselves, 'How can we know when a message has not been spoken by the Lord?' If what a prophet proclaims in the name of the Lord does not take place or come true, that is a message the Lord has not spoken. That prophet has spoken presumptuously. Do not be afraid of him" (Deut. 18:21–22). While this gives us significant help in distinguishing true from false prophets, it does not address the problem entirely. For as we saw earlier, even false prophets can announce a miraculous sign or wonder that *does* come to pass. Moreover, there is also the problem of true prophecy that has not yet been fulfilled. There is no outside time limit provided within which prophecy must be fulfilled, so if a false prophet casts his prophecy sufficiently far into the future, this criterion would not help to identify him. Before proceeding, therefore, we need to consider other ways for determining the legitimacy of a prophetic message declared to be from the Lord.

True Prophets

The Bible provides several ways for us to gauge the legitimacy of a prophetic message. No single criterion is sufficient in itself, and even taken together these criteria are not so comprehensive as to cover every conceivable situation. Nevertheless, these indicators give us invaluable guidance in making our evaluations.

Messengers of Woe. There is always a danger that the prophets are merely seeking to gain favor by saying what their audience wants to hear.[19] Indeed, in Jeremiah 28:8–9 we are told to suspect not the prophet who brings bad news, but rather the one who foretells peace. The prophet who brings bad news has nothing to gain personally from such a message and is therefore far less likely to be fabricating it. That some falsely claim to be prophets in order to benefit from messages of blessing is amply testified in Scripture.[20] This is a sobering reminder to us today. Most of us are fairly comfortable in our routines and pleasures and would quickly change churches if we encountered too many challenges from the pulpit. We would rather be encouraged in our way and trust that God won't be too offended at our failure to address the physical and spiritual needs of others and ourselves. In other words, we would often rather receive a message like what the false prophets gave to their willing listeners among the Israelites. True prophets, however, are willing to engage in the unpleasant business of pointing out the sin of God's people and its con-

19. 2 Tim. 4:2–4.
20. For example, Jer. 23:16–18; Ezek. 13:8–16; Mic. 2:11; 3:5, 11.

sequences, even though such a task means a significant re-
duction in their popularity.

Social Nonconformists. A true prophet goes against the
tide of public opinion, for it is rare for the majority to be
faithfully obeying the demands of the covenant. True
prophets are often resented, mocked, despised, and
ridiculed.[21] Jeremiah, Micaiah, and Hanani were imprisoned
(Jer. 37; 38; 1 Kings 22; 2 Chron. 16); Elijah was forced to
flee (1 Kings 19); and Zechariah was slain (2 Chron.
24:20–22). This treatment continues into the New Testament (Matt. 23:33–37).

True prophets have as their goal, however, not the
praise of the masses, but the approbation of the one who
called them. Their objective is not, therefore, to assimilate
accepted cultural norms, but to challenge those norms
when they conflict with divine standards. This often places
them outside of what is considered socially acceptable and
at odds with those who require such acceptability of every
member of society (that is, those who are intolerant of in-
tolerance).

When we seek to imitate the prophetic functions in our
contemporary situations, we must be ready to face similar
opposition from those who are unready to accept anyone
who follows norms other than those dictated by their society. Indeed, when Jesus prays to the Father concerning his
disciples, he says, "I have given them your word and the
world has hated them, for they are not of the world any more
than I am of the world" (John 17:14). Opposition appears to
be a necessary corollary to a life lived in obedient service to
God. The prophets of the Old Testament were willing (often
only after heavy-duty divine reassurance and coaxing) to ac-

21. 2 Kings 17:13–15; 2 Chron. 36:16; Neh. 9:26; Jer. 25:4; 26:5.

cept this difficult aspect of their calling. If we aspire to such a calling, we too should be aware of the cost.

Traditionalists. I am aware that this is a loaded term these days in the battles that rage in many congregations over worship styles. Those who prefer the older hymns and more formal liturgy are labeled "traditionalists," while those who favor more contemporary choruses and a freer order of worship think of themselves as more progressive (which appears to be an exclusively positive designation). What I am referring to here, however, is that true prophets abide by and promote adherence to antecedent law (dare I say orthodox doctrine?); they do not promote new theology. The prophets call God's people back to the bedrock doctrines of scriptural orthodoxy when the introduction of foreign and heretical elements into their religious life threatens its health. In Jeremiah 6:16–19, God describes his prophets as watchmen who warn his people of the consequences of turning from the "good way" or "ancient paths." These consequences involve nothing less than "disaster":

> This is what the LORD says:
> "Stand at the crossroads and look;
>   ask for the ancient paths,
> ask where the good way is, and walk in it,
>   and you will find rest for your souls.
>   But you said, 'We will not walk in it.'
> I appointed watchmen over you and said,
>   'Listen to the sound of the trumpet!'
>   But you said, 'We will not listen.'
> Therefore hear, O nations;
>   observe, O witnesses,
>   what will happen to them.
> Hear, O earth;

I am bringing disaster on this people,
    the fruit of their schemes,
because they have not listened to my words
    and have rejected my law."

The misguided contemporary notion that prophets generate new theological ideas and directions finds no basis in Scripture. On the contrary, the true prophets call Israel back to the divine law and covenant obligations that she had abandoned.[22] It is no wonder the biblical prophets were so unpopular. In this age too, when entertainment reigns supreme and the popularity of a theological idea depends to a large degree on its departure from traditional norms, contemporary prophets will have a hard job calling for faithfulness to the old, old story. The gospel's relevance to the culture may indeed be demonstrated in a variety of different and exciting ways, but the message, the theology, remains the same. True biblical prophets, therefore, are not inventors of truth or purveyors of novelty, but guardians and promoters of unchanging biblical truth.

Vindicated by Events. One obvious factor that helps to distinguish between true prophets and false ones is that the words of the true prophet are corroborated by their fulfillment. God puts this straightforwardly for the prophet Ezekiel: "When all this comes true—and it surely will—then they will know that a prophet has been among them" (33:33). God alone is in control of history and the unfolding of its events. He alone is able to "foretell what will come" (Isa. 44:6–7):

22. In this connection, Tremper Longman III, *Reading the Bible with Heart and Mind* (Colorado Springs: NavPress, 1997), 169, characterizes prophets as "God's lawyers" who bring "a case against God's people" in order to get the people to return to "their agreement with the one true God—to follow and worship Him."

This is what the LORD says—
Israel's King and Redeemer, the LORD Almighty:
I am the first and I am the last;
apart from me there is no God.
Who then is like me? Let him proclaim it.
Let him declare and lay out before me
what has happened since I established my ancient
people,
and what is yet to come—
yes, let him foretell what will come.

Because God alone is in control of history and the unfolding of its events, he alone is able with absolute accuracy to communicate through his prophets the events that will take place. So, not only is the prophet vindicated by the coming to pass of the events he foretells, but so is God, the one from whom the message originated. The fulfilled prophecy establishes that God does indeed know the end from the beginning, and that the prophet is his bona fide agent.

As we have already seen, however, fulfilled prophecy (like all of the other criteria listed here) is insufficient by itself to distinguish true from false prophets. False prophets may foretell an event that, for a variety of reasons, actually comes to pass. Even a broken clock is correct twice every day. Nevertheless, along with all of the other distinguishing characteristics, a true prophet is also identified when what he foretells comes to pass.

Blameless. Like Samuel (1 Sam. 12:3–5), the true prophets lead exemplary lives. That this is so will be demonstrated in chapter 3 where we examine the whole-life involvement of the prophets in their prophetic task. Their behavior, therefore, is a constituent part of their prophetic message. It is a grievous thing these days when those who claim to be contemporary prophets engage in the very activities they so passionately condemn. This is not to say that only those Christians who are perfect qualify for entrance into the ranks of the prophets. If this were so, the number of eligible candidates would be precisely zero. However, it does mean that the general drift or tenor of a prophet's life should not contradict his message.

The behavior of the false prophets gives the lie to their assertion that they have been in the council of God and called to his service.[23] False prophets are self-serving, not God-serving. Not having actually been called to the prophetic task, they go through their deceptive routines for the purpose of personal enrichment. True prophets, on the other hand, do the right thing even when it hurts (and it usually does). It is clear from the objections the prophets make to their calls that if it were up to them, they would prefer to pursue other vocations. Surely they knew the likely outcome of their calling. Stephen courageously confronts his accusers in the Sanhedrin with his own condemnatory question, which clarifies just how unlikely it was for prophets to be able to look forward to peaceful retirement (Acts 7:52): "Was there ever a prophet your fathers did not persecute? They even killed those who predicted the coming of the Righteous One."[24] It hardly seems the true prophets carried out their appointed tasks for the sake of the job perks. Selfish ambition or vain conceit had no part in their motivation.

The behavioral dimension of the prophetic office is largely neglected these days, but continues to play a significant part in distinguishing between true and false prophets.

---

23. Behavior characterizing the false prophets is described in Isa. 28:7–8; Jer. 23:10–14; Ezek. 13:17–23; Mic. 2:11; 3:5–11.

24. For other passages indicating the harsh treatment of the Lord's prophets, see 1 Kings 19:10; 2 Chron. 36:16; Matt. 5:11–12; 23:37; 1 Thess. 2:15; Heb. 11:32–37.

Whether we admit it or not, unbelievers gauge how strongly we hold our beliefs by how consistently we live them. In these days when the various media command such a large part of so many people's attention, talking heads, talk radio, political sound bites, and other verbal outlets have elevated words to a level where authenticating actions are often ignored. Nevertheless, in real life, actions really do speak louder than words. The prophetic message today, just as in the past, consists of both words and actions in harmony. One who purports to speak words from God should behave in a way that communicates the same message.

CONCLUSION

No single perspective that we have considered is able fully to account for the complicated lives and missions of the biblical characters called prophets. To focus on one or another dimension of the prophetic office to the exclusion of the others results in a distorted and even dangerous understanding of the essential prophetic task. Contemporary applications of such misunderstandings may cause severe damage in the church and harm the Christian witness in the world (as has been the case too many times in the past). Our distillation of both the scriptural guidelines and the manifold perspectives produced from years of study and reflection must faithfully incorporate all of these factors while rejecting any overemphases in human perceptions that might distort our subsequent application—a tall order! Before we try to boil down this information into something usable, let's review our findings in this chapter:

1. The biblical terminology used for the prophets indicates that they "see" things usually not perceived by others.

2. The prophet has been called by God to perform his task.
3. God enables prophets to speak and act as he desires.
4. The prophets may communicate in ways that are difficult to understand.
5. True prophets may be identified by messages that are often unpopular, go against predominant cultural patterns, promote scriptural orthodoxy, and are corroborated by events.
6. The behavior of prophets communicates the same message as do their words.

We must combine these insights with those of chapter 1 in order to formulate a basic perspective from which we may begin to examine the specific activities of the prophets. With modern technology enabling us to cut and paste with ease, it would be tempting for us to paste together a giant amalgam of everything we have considered—a veritable super paragraph describing the essence of a prophet. This, however, would hardly do us any good. What is necessary is a simple, usable, and accurate rubric that captures all of the different facets of the prophetic persona.

There is a tool we can use to shave our super paragraph down to size—Occam's razor. This term is used to describe a principle formulated by the fourteenth-century English philosopher, William of Occam (it is also called the law of parsimony). This principle requires that "any scientific explanation be based on the fewest possible assumptions necessary to account adequately for all the facts involved,"[25] or, in Occam's own words: "Entities [of explanation] are not to be multiplied beyond need."[26]

---

25. Alburey Castell and Donald M. Borchert, *An Introduction to Modern Philosophy: Examining the Human Condition* (New York: Macmillan, 1983), 147.
26. Ibid.

Applying this principle to our analysis results in a description of a prophet that is simple, and yet includes within it elements of all of the various features of the prophetic office we have considered. It includes the prophetic responsibility to communicate faithfully the message received from the Lord, as well as the responsibility the prophet bears to the community of which he is a member. It involves the prophet's words, behavior, affections—indeed everything about the prophet as a human being. This perspective of the essential prophetic task that will shape all of our subsequent considerations of his individual, specific actions is that the prophet is fundamentally *a representative*. He represents God, the community of which he is a part, and, of course, himself in ways that are unique to this special office he occupies. Having said this, we might well conclude that we have shaved our working perspective a little too close. But this is not the case. As we will see in the next chapter, where we examine what a prophet does, this apparently simple perspective encompasses an extremely complex and interactive matrix of responsibilities that demand the full-time engagement of the prophet's entire being. What this means in practical terms leads us to the next stage of our investigation.

FOR FURTHER REFLECTION

1. How do the words used for "prophet" in the Bible help us to understand this biblical figure?
2. What parallels do you see between the elements of the divine call and your own spiritual journey?
3. Explain why prophetic texts may be more difficult to comprehend than other biblical texts. How should this affect the way you read them?

THREE

WHAT A PROPHET DOES

Having proposed that the basic function of a prophet is that of a representative, in this chapter we will see how all of the individual actions of a prophet can be easily understood from this primary perspective. We will examine each prophetic representative function in turn and support our conclusions with scriptural examples.

A PROPHET REPRESENTS GOD

We begin our analysis with that dimension of the prophet's representative function that finds the greatest witness in the scholarly treatments of this biblical character. Even though this dimension more than any other has been dealt with in studies of the prophets, it is more complicated than is usually realized because the prophet does not just represent God verbally, with words, but with the totality of his being. While the prophet's verbal representation of God is well discussed in the literature, there is a surprising lack of attention paid to the other means by which he carries out his responsibility to communicate the divine message. In the discussion that follows, we begin with the familiar before progressing down less well known avenues.

Verbally

We hardly need to spend much time establishing that a significant part of the prophetic task is to represent God with words. The prophetic texts abound with familiar phrases such as "Thus says the LORD," "The LORD said to me," or "The word of the LORD came to. . . ." All of these phrases indicate that what follows will be a verbal expression of the divine revelation that the prophet receives (in some mysterious way). But exactly how the prophet comes into possession of this divine revelation remains shrouded in mystery. Scripture indicates, in general terms, some of the ways this transmission takes place, even if the precise mechanisms involved remain obscure.

One way that the divine revelation is communicated to the prophet is through dreams or visions. It is not certain that these are the same thing, but our understanding of their nature is too incomplete to draw any clear distinction between them. In Deuteronomy 13:1 the term "prophet" is used in parallel with "one who foretells by dreams": "If a prophet, or one who foretells by dreams, appears among you . . ." Moreover, as we saw earlier, God himself states that he reveals himself to prophets in dreams and visions (Num. 12:6). When Saul sought a word from the Lord regarding his battle with the Philistines, the Lord refused to answer him by dreams. This clearly indicates that dreams are one way that God communicates his will. In the famous eschatological prophecy of Joel 2:28–32, prophesying is paralleled with dreaming dreams and seeing visions (v. 28):

And afterward,
   I will pour out my Spirit on all people.
Your sons and daughters will *prophesy,*

your old men will *dream dreams,*
your young men will *see visions.*

False prophets are able to deceive the people by declaring that their revelation comes by way of a dream (Jer. 23:25–32). This fraud would hardly be effective if dreams were not a usual means for God to make his will known to the prophets. Geerhardus Vos, however, maintains that dreams are a second-class avenue for divine revelation reserved for those who don't rate some more direct revelation:

> In dreaming, the consciousness of the dreamer is more or less loosened from his personality. Hence dreams were preferably used as a vehicle of revelation where the spiritual state was ill-adapted for contact with God. In this way the unfit personality was to some extent neutralized, and the mind was a mere receptacle of the message. Heathen persons receive revelation through this medium. Within the chosen family, dreams were utilized likewise where the spirituality of the person was immature or at a low ebb.[1]

This goes well beyond what the biblical evidence allows. It is true that such unbelievers as Pharaoh (Gen. 41) and non-Jews like Cornelius (Acts 10) have dreams or visions. But so do Joseph (Gen. 37) and Peter (Acts 11), and we are not told that their spiritual state is anything other than healthy. Additionally, none of the passages we considered above that discuss God using this means of revealing his will to his prophets hints that this mode of revelation is reserved for those at some spiritual low point. However, even granting

1. Geerhardus Vos, *Biblical Theology: Old and New Testaments* (Grand Rapids: Eerdmans, 1948), 85.

that this is only one of several means for God to communicate to his prophets, we are still left with very little understanding of precisely what it entails. This leaves our curiosity
not entirely satisfied, and I regret to report that we have even
less information regarding the next mode of revelation we
will be considering.

We learn from the Scriptures of a strange experience
that is limited to true prophets and that is apparently,
though mysteriously, at least occasionally a means of
prophetic revelation. It is called the *sod yhwh* (סוֹד יהוה), or
the council of the LORD, and consists of the heavenly as-
sembly of the Lord and his angels.[2] It is apparently the same
celestial gathering witnessed by Isaiah in his vision of the
Lord, seated on his throne, surrounded by his attendant,
worshiping seraphim (Isa. 6:1–4).[3] We get another glimpse
of this mysterious phenomenon in 1 Kings 22:19–22, where
the prophet Micaiah recounts to Ahab and Jehoshaphat, the
kings of Israel and Judah, his vision of "the LORD sitting on
his throne with all the host of heaven standing around him
on his right and on his left." The Lord consults with this
"host of heaven" before deciding on a specific course of action. Micaiah had been granted a special privileged vision of
this process so that he could make God's decision concerning Ahab known.

God also makes it clear through the prophet Jeremiah
that such revelation is reserved for true prophets alone. In
his gracious appeal to his people to abandon their misguided
reliance upon the words of the false prophets, God points
out that the false prophets have never stood in the council of
the Lord:

---

2. Heinz-Josef Fabry, "סוֹד," *TDOT,* 10:171–78; and M. Saebø, "סוֹד *sôd* secret,"
TLOT, 2:793–95.

3. John D. W. Watts, *Isaiah 1–33*, Word Biblical Commentary, vol. 24 (Waco,
Tex.: Word, 1985), 70–75.

Do not listen to what the prophets are prophesying
   to you;
  they fill you with false hopes.
They speak visions from their own minds,
  not from the mouth of the LORD.
They keep saying to those who despise me,
  "The LORD says: You will have peace."
And to all who follow the stubbornness of their
   hearts
  they say, "No harm will come to you."
But which of them has stood in the council of the
   LORD
  to see or to hear his word?
  Who has listened and heard his word? (Jer.
   23:16–18)

This prophetic access to the divine council may even explain the response given when Elisha asks to inherit Elijah's prophetic mantle. Elijah says that if Elisha is granted a vision of the heavenly goings-on when he, Elijah, is taken up into heaven, that would be a sufficient indicator that Elisha had been divinely designated as a true, legitimate prophet (2 Kings 2:9–15).

A far more common means of the prophets' reception of the divine message, though, once again, no better understood, is the revelatory activity of the Holy Spirit. In the confrontation between the true prophet Micaiah and the false prophet Zedekiah described in 1 Kings 22:24, Zedekiah falsely claims to have been inspired by the Spirit, but his words at least reveal that he realizes such inspiration is requisite for true prophecy: "Which way did the Spirit of the LORD go when he went from me to speak to you?" In another passage, the prophet Micah asserts that his reception of the Spirit was for the express purpose of making known the word of God: "I am filled with power, with the Spirit of the LORD . . . to declare to Jacob his transgression, to Israel his sin" (Mic. 3:8). Similarly, the prophet Zechariah clearly explains that God sends his word to his prophets by his Spirit: "They . . . would not listen to the law or the words that the LORD Almighty had sent by his Spirit through the earlier prophets" (Zech. 7:12). In the New Testament, this mysterious process is referred to again by Peter: "Prophecy never had its origin in the will of man, but men spoke from God as they were carried along by the Holy Spirit" (2 Peter 1:21).

Finally, the most common way in which a prophet received a divine revelation was simply that "the word of the LORD came to" him. This is succinctly stated without further elaboration, leaving us to wonder what exactly has happened. The word translated "came" is simply the "to be" verb in Hebrew. We could therefore just as accurately translate this phrase "the word of the LORD 'happened' to" the prophet. In other words, the divine word just "was."

Because none of these means that we find in Scripture is accompanied by a detailed explanation of its particulars, we must conclude that this is not an area that God intends for us to know with any specificity. Consequently, we move from this rather unfruitful avenue of exploration to a more objective and productive field of investigation involving the verbal dimension of the prophet's representation of God: the forms of that verbal communication.

Entire books have been written on the forms of prophetic speech,[4] and we need not reproduce those efforts here. We will content ourselves in our present study with a brief listing and description of the generally accepted forms

---

4. See, for example, Claus Westermann, *Basic Forms of Prophetic Speech,* trans. Hugh Clayton White (Louisville: Westminster/John Knox, 1991); and Klaus Koch, *The Growth of the Biblical Tradition: The Form-Critical Method* (New York: Macmillan, 1969).

of prophetic speech, while noting that the lines between these forms are not rigidly drawn; there is some overlap. The forms or structures of these verbal prophetic communications are inextricably bound to their content in the same way that a contemporary letter beginning with "Dear John" may provide the recipient with a clue to its unwelcome content. Claus Westermann lists three basic types or genres of prophetic communication: accounts, speeches, and prayers.

Accounts include the third-person narratives comprising the historical material of the prophetic books. These consist of superscriptions, notations concerning the time and/or place of a prophetic speech or experience, and reports of prophetic conflicts, actions, or calls. These historical and biographical materials constitute a significant percentage of the prophetic books, but have not received anything approaching the attention given to the actual speeches of the prophets. Nevertheless, their significance is not for that reason any less, and we will devote appropriate attention to them below.

The prophetic speeches comprise the actual words of the prophets as delivered to their intended recipients. These are usually subdivided logically into prophetic judgment speeches and prophetic salvation speeches. The prophetic judgment speeches may be directed toward individuals or nations and contain two main parts: the accusation (in which the particular offense or offenses are listed) and the announcement of judgment.[5] The prophetic salvation speeches are less structured and yet are easily identified on the basis of their content. These speeches frequently orient the hearer to the promised day of salvation by beginning

5. For a description and examples of the form of a prophetic judgment speech against individuals or nations, see Westermann, *Basic Forms of Prophetic Speech*, 129–62, 169–89.

with a phrase such as "in that day" or "the days are coming." Examples include Isaiah 2:2–5; 4:2–6; 7:7–9; Jeremiah 28:2–4; 33:10–13; Amos 9:11–12, 13–15; and Micah 4:1–4; 5:7–9, 10–15.

The prayers found in the prophetic books are strikingly similar to those in the book of Psalms. They include both prayers of praise (e.g., Amos 4:13; 5:8–9; 9:5–6) and prayers of lament (e.g., Jer. 11:18–12:6; 15:10–21). These prayers give us insight into the mind-set of the prophet, helping us to understand what concerns him or gives him joy, but they do much more than that. This isn't the communication of the prophetic message as we have been trained to understand it. This is a communication of a different sort, although still using words. It is not directed toward us, but rather to God. Nevertheless, by letting us peek into this intimate conversation, the divine author of Scripture has perhaps without our knowledge continued to communicate a message to us. This form of communication begins to shade into the "behavioral" type we discuss below. Let us begin to consider this more indirect type of communication by looking at some obvious examples and then proceeding to a consideration of other, subtler means.

Behaviorally

We don't get very far at all in our reading of any prophetic book of the Old Testament before realizing that not everything we read is a formal pronouncement of the prophet. There is much material written in the third person *about* the prophet, describing his actions. At times we are even given glimpses of the prophet's emotional state as he speaks or acts—we have already begun to see this in our brief consideration of the prophetic prayers. What we too often fail to realize is that these other perspectives that we observe in the text concerning the prophet are themselves also an intended part of the prophetic communication, contributing their part to the special, redemptive revelation of God contained within the prophet's message. Today we are very familiar with the concept of body language—that we are able to communicate all sorts of information without uttering a single word just by the way we physically position ourselves. We need to grow in our ability to receive and decode from the prophetic texts the same type of communication that regularly confronts us in nonverbal ways in our contemporary situations. The Scripture itself frequently reminds us that its message is not only for those who have "ears to hear"—implying a verbal communication—but also for those who have "eyes to see"—implying a communication that is acted out and therefore visible.

The prophets behaviorally communicate their message from God in a variety of ways. It is important to notice that these physical activities never occur in isolation from the spoken word. They are performed together with the spoken word in order to enhance visually, to substantiate, or to demonstrate its content. One variety of this nonverbal communication involves the performance of symbolic acts. These acts may be performed by the prophet himself or on his behalf,[6] but in either case they are an important part of the message he is communicating. Though the examples of these symbolic acts are surprisingly numerous in the prophetic texts, for the sake of brevity we will provide here only a few examples to demonstrate these extraordinary phenomena.[7]

6. Evans, *Prophets of the Lord*, 28: "In several of the prophetic books we find accounts of actions performed by the prophet or on his behalf. These actions are symbolic of the way in which God intends to act toward his people."

7. For more examples of prophetic communication by means of behavior, see Kelvin G. Friebel, *Jeremiah's and Ezekiel's Sign-Acts: Rhetorical Non-verbal Communication*, JSOTSup 283 (Sheffield: Sheffield Academic Press, 1999), and Stacey, *Prophetic Drama in the Old Testament*.

In Jeremiah 18, the Lord instructs Jeremiah to go to the potter's house, where the potter is molding his medium however he wishes. There, with the visual picture of the potter's freedom to shape the pot on his wheel "as seemed best to him," God communicates to Israel his ability to deal similarly with them in response to their behavior, as seems best to him: "O house of Israel, can I not do with you as this potter does?" (v. 6).

Later, in chapter 19, when the people of Judah have made it clear that they would not obey the law of the Lord, he instructs Jeremiah to communicate his message of judgment to them both verbally and behaviorally. The behavioral component involves the prophet's smashing a clay jar, as was done in connection with ancient Near Eastern execration oaths,[8] *while the elders and the priests were watching.* These execration oaths involved writing the names of one's enemies or other unpleasant things such as illness or defraudment on a clay pot, and then smashing it in the belief that the written things would similarly be destroyed or avoided. It is important to note that the elders and priests were not only to hear Jeremiah's words, but also to see the message acted out in a way in which they could not possibly misinterpret its meaning. By smashing the pot while they were watching, Jeremiah effectively and dramatically conveyed God's message that he would "smash this nation and this city just as this potter's jar is smashed and cannot be repaired" (Jer. 19:11).

Among the many symbolic acts Ezekiel performs, we may point to that found in Ezekiel 5:1–4, where the Lord directs Ezekiel to shave his head and beard with a sharp sword. A third of this hair he is to burn, a third he is to strike with the sword, and a third he is to scatter to the wind—saving

8. For examples of such oaths, see John A. Wilson, "The Execration of Asiatic Princes," *ANET,* 328–29.

only a few strands from such abuse. Anyone unaccustomed to the behavioral dimension of prophetic representation may have been a little alarmed at this unusual behavior. However, this act complemented Ezekiel's verbal communication and symbolized what the Lord was going to do to his people by means of Assyria, "a razor hired from beyond the River" (Isa. 7:20).

We must also include in our list of behavioral representation the pitiable life of Hosea the prophet, whose marriage to unfaithful Gomer provides a graphic picture of Israel's own unfaithfulness to God. Here again we begin to see an expansion of our narrowly defined categories, because the prophets do not represent God by means of symbolic actions that are without any actual personal investment. It is not as though they are performing a dramatic skit, after which they return to their seat in the temple. The prophets' lives in their entirety are used by God as virtual living billboards that advertise his intentions. In contemporary language, the prophetic task is 24/7. No vacations, sabbaticals, or interludes.

Thus we must examine every detail of the prophets' lives for its revelatory potential. We must be careful not to neglect any aspect of their communication, as it has been recorded for us in the Scriptures, and not to focus just on those aspects that fit best with our societal norms or expectations. One much neglected aspect of the prophets' lives to which we must also give some careful attention is their affections.

Affectively

A prophet communicates his message from God not only by his words and behaviors, but also by his affections. "Affections" is an old-fashioned word that is nevertheless very appropriate to describe this aspect of prophetic representation. The word means "an affecting or moving of the mind in any way; a mental state brought about by any influ-ence; an emotion or feeling"; or even "state of mind gener-ally, mental tendency, disposition."[9] It may also refer more broadly to "a bodily state" such as hunger or thirst.[10] I use the term here, therefore, to indicate all those internal, pre-dominantly nonvisible, nonverbal aspects of a human being that are described for us in the Scriptures. Even these as-pects of a prophet are occasionally used in a representational capacity to communicate something to us about God.

The prophet Jeremiah, for example, has often been called "the weeping prophet" because of the great emotion he exhibits in his prophecy. We see an instance of his tremen-dous sadness in Jeremiah 13:15–17, where he describes his bitter sorrow over his people's refusal to listen responsively to the word of God. While this is no doubt a real emotion of Jeremiah's, it is also representative of the emotion that God himself is experiencing at this critical time in the life of his people, when their continued existence as a nation in the Promised Land is in extreme jeopardy. We also see this di-vine emotion displayed in such passages as Jeremiah 14:17–18, where God instructs Jeremiah to say to his peo-ple: "Let my eyes overflow with tears night and day without ceasing; for my virgin daughter—my people—has suffered a grievous wound, a crushing blow." In these words we see the tremendous pathos of our compassionate God, whose care for his people overflows in anguished words from his prophet's mouth. Jeremiah is the weeping prophet because he is manifesting God's own sorrow over the judgment he must bring upon his beloved people.

On the other end of the emotional spectrum, we have the fiery prophet Amos, who demonstrates God's anger

---

9. *The Compact Oxford English Dictionary*, 2d ed. (Oxford: Clarendon, 1991), 24.
10. Ibid.

against Israel with such outbursts as: "The LORD roars from Zion and thunders from Jerusalem; the pastures of the shepherds dry up, and the top of Carmel withers" (Amos 1:2). And who can miss the divine outrage in Amos's pronouncements against Israel's empty sacrifices: "I hate, I despise your religious feasts; I cannot stand your assemblies. Even though you bring me burnt offerings and grain offerings, I will not accept them. . . . Away with the noise of your songs! I will not listen to the music of your harps" (Amos 5:21–23). I am absolutely certain that Amos did not deliver these words with the monotone emotionless droning characteristic of a line-by-line explanation of a 253-item annual budget (my apologies to accountants everywhere)! No doubt his face was red, his voice was elevated, and his actions animated. Certainly Amos was like that, but the point he was making was that the Lord was expressing these emotions too! If the people wanted to know how exercised the Lord was about their sin, they could look at Amos and *see* as well as hear.

A visible demonstration of God's unrequited love for his people is Hosea's dysfunctional relationship with his disloyal wife Gomer: "The LORD said to me, 'Go, show your love to your wife again, though she is loved by another and is an adulteress. Love her as the LORD loves the Israelites, though they turn to other gods and love the sacred raisin cakes'" (Hos. 3:1). Those who followed the soap-opera-like goings-on between blameless Hosea and his fickle and faithless wife were meant to recognize in the drama played out before them their own spiritual adultery. Hosea's visible heartbreak and disappointment with his wife testified also to God's own displeasure at his people's behavior. Yet God in his wonderful grace and mercy still loved his people and desired a relationship with them. He visually displayed this forgiving love by means of Hosea's continued love for Gomer despite her untrustworthiness.

When the prophet Micah declares that because of the sin of God's people "I will weep and wail; I will go about barefoot and naked. I will howl like a jackal and moan like an owl" (Mic. 1:8), exactly whose emotions are we seeing? The prophet's? Or God's? Here again, God intends for us to see in the extreme emotion of this prophet the profound depth of his sorrow over the broken relationship with his people.

We see once again that it is not only the *words* of the prophets that have revelational content, but also their *affections*. Their emotions, attitudes, outlooks, opinions, and general dispositions all have been recorded for us in the inspired text because these too are "useful for teaching, rebuking, correcting, and training in righteousness" (2 Tim. 3:16). Our understanding of the contemporary application of the prophetic task to the church today must not fail to include the affective dimension. It was and is a vital component of prophetic communication.

Completely

Having analyzed the variety of representational aspects of the prophetic task, we arrive at the comprehensive and rather bold conclusion that the prophets are, in effect, preincarnational manifestations of God. That is, before the incarnation of Christ, God communicates his message in manifold ways through his servants, the prophets.[11] Everything about their lives contributed to the divine message they were being used to convey. For them the transmission of God's will to those "with eyes to see and ears to hear" was not simply a nine-to-five job. It involved every aspect of the prophets' lives and re-

---

11. Or, in words that are perhaps a little more crude, but no less accurate, Sunday Aigbe, "A Biblical Foundation for the Prophetic Mandate," *Pneuma* 11/2 (1989): 88, puts it this way: "The prophets were the 'little Yahwehs' who physically met the people in their situation for the invisible 'Big Yahweh.' "

quired their complete involvement in the task.[12] Yes, the spoken word was important. But this verbal communication was
supplemented, enhanced, corroborated, demonstrated, and
embodied by their behaviors and affections.

Even though we have considered the various aspects of
prophetic representation separately, we should be careful to
note that this was for convenience only. In reality, these various dimensions of the prophets' lives can no more be separated than they can be in our own lives. All of these methods
of communication operate simultaneously in every healthy human being. Can you imagine a marriage proposal given with a
yawn? Or how about words of appreciation shouted while one
is waving one's fists in the air? These things just don't go together. We know this in our personal lives, but somehow we
are prone to forget it when we consider the lives of the
prophets. We tend to focus on propositional truths expressed
with words, while overlooking the other significant communication accompanying those words. Our perception of the message becomes immensely richer as we sensitize ourselves to
these other types of communication. Moreover, as we apply
these prophetic representational tasks to our own contemporary situations, we must take into account the practical implications and demands of this all-encompassing responsibility to
communicate God's message with the entirety of our beings.

A PROPHET REPRESENTS
HIS COMMUNITY

While the prophetic representational task seems to be
complicated enough already, there is still much more to con-

---

12. Stacey, *Prophetic Drama in the Old Testament,* 66: "The prophets knew nothing of professional detachment; they were, or wished to be thought to be, totally involved in their work."

sider, because a prophet's representational responsibilities are far more complex than the simple unidirectional communication we have been considering; that is, from God to humankind. The prophet also has a representational responsibility to his community, to communicate on their behalf. Just as a prophet cannot separate the various aspects of his personality from his prophetic witness, he cannot separate himself from the community of which he is a part—nor did God intend for him to do so.[13] An important part of the prophet's task involves representing his own community, and it should come as no surprise by now to learn that he carries out this responsibility with all of the aspects of his personality that he uses in his representation of God—with his words, his behavior, and his affections. Just as we did for each of the means by which a prophet represents God, we will examine each of the means by which a prophet represents his community.

Verbally

In chapter 1 we observed that, among other things, the prophet has a mediatorial role that is well attested in Scripture. Not only does he represent God to those who receive his message, but he also represents his community to God. He accomplishes this task verbally by means of prayer. When the prophet speaks to God, he may be speaking on behalf of or as a representative of his community. Thus, intercessory prayer is a very common example of the way in which a prophet carries out this task of representing his community

---

13. Evans, *Prophets of the Lord*, 19–20: "Nor should we see a prophet's work as consisting only of bringing messages from God. . . . They were also responsible to pray for the people, and *by the way they lived out their own lives to show what it meant to be in relationship with God*" (emphasis added).

verbally.[14] We may consider here just a few examples of such prophetic intercession.

Moses, the paradigm prophet,[15] intercedes for the people after their idolatry with the golden calf and thereby averts God's wrath against them (Exod. 32:30–34; Ps. 106:23). Later, Moses intercedes with the Lord on behalf of disputatious Miriam, who is subsequently healed of her leprosy (Num. 12). Samuel intercedes for the community after they have fallen under Philistine domination (1 Sam. 7:5–13) and again later when they ask for a king (1 Sam. 12:18–23). Amos effectively prays that God would spare Israel from the disasters he had planned for them (Amos 7:1–6).

This intercessory responsibility of the prophets was recognized by the royal administration. When the northern kingdom of Israel was besieged by the seemingly insuperable Assyrian military machine, King Hezekiah responded to the threat by sending a delegation to the prophet Isaiah seeking his intercessory prayer for the kingdom (Isa. 37:1–4). This gave clear testimony to Hezekiah's conviction that this task of intercession was one of the primary responsibilities of prophets—a conviction that subsequent events proved to be well founded. Even the vacillating King Zedekiah knew enough to send a delegation to the prophet Jeremiah with the message, "Please pray to the LORD our God for us" (Jer. 37:3).

---

14. Freedman, "Between God and Man," 70: "In addition to the primary task of the prophet as messenger and spokesman for God, mention should also be made of another at least equally important role: intercessor on behalf of the people of God." We hasten to add, however, that while the prophets focus their attention on the covenant community, their intercession is not limited to that group. Abraham prays for Abimelech (Gen. 20:7) and Moses for Pharaoh (Exod. 8:8, 12, 28–30; 9:28–33; 10:16–18).

15. Koch, *The Prophets*, 1:16: "For Jews and Christians alike, Moses counts as being the prototype of a prophet."

When the gracious opportunity for his people to repent
has passed, God deletes this vital task of intercession from
the prophetic job description. Thus, when judgment upon
Judah has become inevitable, God forbids Jeremiah from
carrying out his prophetic responsibility to intercede for the
people (Jer. 7:16; 14:11). The power and significance of this
divine prohibition would be minimal indeed if this were not
an ordinary and expected function of a true prophet. Conversely, false prophets exposed the illegitimacy of their
claims to the prophetic office by their failure to pray for the
people. Concerning the false prophets in Jerusalem just
prior to Judah's demise, the Lord says: "I looked for a man
among them who would build up the wall and stand before
me in the gap on behalf of the land so I would not have to
destroy it, but I found none" (Ezek. 22:30).

The fundamental selfishness of false prophets manifests
itself in their failure to pray for their community. Anyone
who undertakes to carry out the prophetic tasks in the
church today should take careful note of this weighty responsibility to intercede for God's people.

Behaviorally

As we would now expect, a prophet's responsibility to
represent his community to God is not restricted to words.
A prophet indicates what will happen to his community by
experiencing those things himself, symbolically or literally.

Just as a prophet could use symbolic acts to demonstrate
visually the message he was delivering from God, in the
same way a prophet could use symbolic acts to demonstrate
visually to his community the circumstances they would encounter in the future. For example, Ezekiel wordlessly acts
out the conditions that would exist within Jerusalem during
the coming siege (Ezek. 4:9–17). He, representing his community's coming *experience,* rations out food for himself in

order to show that "the people will eat rationed food in anx-
iety and drink rationed water in despair, for food and water
will be scarce" (vv. 16–17).

In another instance of prophetic, dramatic enactment,
Ezekiel symbolically goes into exile to demonstrate to the
people what they would soon be doing. In this passage, note
how many times God expressly commands Ezekiel to perform these representational actions *while they are watching:*

> Therefore, son of man, pack your belongings for ex-
> ile and in the daytime, *as they watch,* set out and go
> from where you are to another place. Perhaps they
> will understand, though they are a rebellious house.
> During the daytime, *while they watch,* bring out your
> belongings packed for exile. Then in the evening,
> *while they are watching,* go out like those who go into
> exile. *While they watch,* dig through the wall and take
> your belongings out through it. Put them on your
> shoulder *while they are watching* and carry them out
> at dusk. Cover your face so that you cannot see the
> land, for I have made you a sign to the house of Is-
> rael. (Ezek. 12:3–6)

Similarly, the Lord instructs Jeremiah to "make a yoke
out of straps and crossbars" and put it on his neck (Jer. 27:2)
in order to show his people[16] that they would soon be under
the yoke of the Babylonians. Those unable to hear Jeremiah's
words regarding the coming judgment would surely understand the performance acted out before their very eyes.

---

16. This demonstration is not only for the people of God, but also for the kings
of Edom, Moab, Ammon, Tyre, and Sidon (Jer. 27:3). Just as the prophetic representation of God is not limited to his people, the prophetic representation of humanity is not limited to the people of God, though focusing on them.

It is beyond dispute that the prophets' messages had a *visual* component as well as a *verbal* one, and anyone with eyes to see would be able to understand. We are perhaps comfortable and relatively familiar with this symbolic kind of behavioral representation and have little difficulty in accepting it in light of the many obvious examples in Scripture.[17] A second kind of behavioral representation—foretelling by actual representational experience—is perhaps less familiar and requires a bit more explanation. The first kind of behavioral communication involves symbolic acts; that is, acts that the prophet performs that point toward something else. Jeremiah's yoke, for example, points toward the yoke of captivity; it is not captivity itself. Ezekiel's symbolic exile points toward the coming real exile even if it is not a real exile itself. The second kind of behavioral communication, however, involves the prophet in an actual experience of exactly what the people will experience. It is not symbolic. It is a foretaste experienced by the prophet as a sort of preview of what is coming for the nation as a whole. In experiencing this foretaste, the prophet is, in effect, standing in place of the nation. He, in his individual person, is undergoing experiences as though he were the entire community of God's people in miniature. What he actually experiences the nation as a whole will actually experience. His life then becomes a veritable billboard on which God posts his notices. Let us look at a few examples from the life of the prophet who re-

---

17. To this type of symbolic communication, Rofé, *Introduction to the Prophetic Literature,* would add those times when the prophet's message includes a concrete illustration or example: "Symbolic acts can clearly be divided into two categories. The one is no more than an illustration serving to prove the prophet's assertion [e.g., the Rechabites in Jer. 35]. . . . Of a very different kind is the story about the yoke Jeremiah was told to put on his neck (27:2, 12; 28). Here . . . the symbolic act is a foreshadowing of a situation about to take place" (71–72). However, an illustration is hardly a symbol, and Rofé appears to be mixing categories here.

ceives the most extensive narrative treatment—the prophet Jeremiah.

The Lord forbids Jeremiah to marry and have children (Jer. 16:1–4) in order to demonstrate by means of his actual experience that in the future there would be no sons and daughters (nor parents) in the entire land; that is, there would be no more marriages or new births for *anyone*. Furthermore, Jeremiah was not permitted to participate in feasting and drinking in order to indicate the coming removal of all celebration from the land. God tells Jeremiah that he must behave in this way to show that "before your eyes and in your days I will bring an end to the sounds of joy and gladness and to the voices of bride and bridegroom in this place" (Jer. 16:8–9).

The organizing principle for the book of Jeremiah has long been a source of scholarly puzzlement. Yet the reason behind the juxtaposition of at least some chapters in the book becomes immediately apparent when we consider the prophet's experience as representative of the nation as a whole. The imprisonment of Jeremiah, for example, is an event that can open up for us a fresh new way to comprehend his message for the nation. In chapters 37–38 Jeremiah is imprisoned and then thrown into a cistern where he is in real danger of losing his life. He is subsequently delivered from the cistern but "remained in the courtyard of the guard until the day Jerusalem was captured" (38:28). In the very next chapter (39), Jerusalem falls and the nation goes into exile—a prison of sorts—where they are in real danger of disappearing from history. Jeremiah's actual individual experience has therefore precisely foreshadowed the experience of the nation as a whole. As a positive postscript we may also add that just as Jeremiah is finally released from prison, so the nation itself can look forward to their own ultimate release from captivity, even as they head into exile.

On this same positive note, earlier Jeremiah was instructed by God to buy a field in Anathoth from his cousin Hanamel (Jer. 32:6–7). Now on the face of it this appears to have been an extremely illogical command. The Babylonians were overrunning the country, and the value of personal real estate must surely have been in serious question. To any outside observer (and most inside ones, too) it would have seemed all but certain that the life of Judah as a separate nation with territorial possession was over. The idea that somehow personal real estate claims outlined on deeds would ever be honored in the future appeared highly unlikely, to say the least. Yet Jeremiah was commanded to purchase a field and go through the necessary paperwork to demonstrate *in his actual experience* that "houses, fields, and vineyards will again be bought in this land" (Jer. 32:15). So even those in Judah who refused to listen to the prophet's words could understand the implications of his message for them by simply regarding the experiences of his life.

Thus, not only by their words, but also by their actual experiences, the prophets engage in their task of representing the people of God. But the prophets are not mere automatons who perform their roles without any personal investment. The prophetic task of representing the people of God requires nothing less than the full participation of the prophets in every aspect of their being—even those aspects not necessarily characterized by words or behaviors. We therefore turn now to a consideration of a neglected revelatory dimension of the prophet's persona—his affections.

Affectively

Sometimes we forget the rather obvious fact that the prophet himself is also a member of the community of God's people. He does not exist or function in isolation from his countrymen, but is intimately related to his community politically, religiously, and even genetically. The prophet's message to his kinsmen carries with it implications not only for them, but for himself as well. The recorded testimony of how the divine message affects the prophet individually is also prophetically significant and constitutes an important, but often overlooked, part of that message itself. Just as the community of God's people could look to the prophet, in the ways we have previously discussed, for a verbal and behavioral revelation of God, so also could they look to the prophet to see a microcosm of themselves from an affective perspective. In other words, even the prophet's personal affections reveal something about the community he represents, whether favorable or unfavorable.

Let's look again at the prophet Jeremiah to see how he represents his people in this way. In Jeremiah 8:18–19, Jeremiah expresses his own inner turmoil at the devastation befalling his land and his yearning for divine saving intervention. His emotion-laden words exactly embody the turmoil of the people he represents: "O my Comforter in sorrow, my heart is faint within me. Listen to the cry of my people from a land far away: 'Is the LORD not in Zion? Is her King no longer there?' "

The prophet Micah too describes a misery that is felt not only by him, but by the entire nation he represents: "What misery is mine! I am like one who gathers summer fruit at the gleaning of the vineyard; there is no cluster of grapes to eat, none of the early figs that I crave. . . . But as for me, I watch in hope for the LORD, I wait for God my Savior; my God will hear me" (Mic. 7:1, 7). Micah continues to speak in the first person, yet is clearly speaking for the nation as a whole, as he looks forward to the salvation of God he anticipated earlier:

> Do not gloat over me, my enemy!
> Though I have fallen, I will rise.

Though I sit in darkness,
   the LORD will be my light.
Because I have sinned against him,
   I will bear the LORD's wrath,
until he pleads my case
   and establishes my right.
He will bring me out into the light;
   I will see his righteousness.
Then my enemy will see it
   and will be covered with shame,
she who said to me,
   "Where is the LORD your God?"
My eyes will see her downfall;
   even now she will be trampled underfoot
   like mire in the streets. (Mic. 7:8–10)

The affections that we see communicated in the prophetic texts are a significant part of the revelation God intends for us to receive and to comprehend. The truth of God's redemptive plan could have been revealed to us in exclusively objective propositions, but thankfully it wasn't! What we find instead in the pages of Scripture is a communication that addresses the entirety of our makeup as human beings. In our computerized age, we have grown to accept the fact that communication equals data. However, in our personal interactions we show that we understand otherwise. We need to make an effort to apply that understanding to the biblical prophetic texts and give adequate regard to their more subjective dimensions as well. For even though the prophetic texts are sometimes regarded as if they were only hodgepodges of inconsequential historical and verbal debris from which only occasionally gems of biblical truth may be mined, we have seen that the reality is far different. The prophets' lives in all of their complex fullness and in all of their recorded detail embody their message. Thus, not only direct prophetic speeches, but also accounts of the prophets' behaviors and descriptions of their inner lives are significant revelation that we must grow more skilled in translating.

Completely

Once again, because of the requirements of this systematic examination of complex biblical personalities, we have considered separately several aspects of a prophet's life that cannot exist that way in actual experience. A prophet is a constituent member of the society that receives his message. He is not able to divorce himself from his community to fulfill his prophetic calling, nor is he expected to do so. In fact, representing the community is a fundamental part of what it means to be a prophet. The complicated task of the prophet requires him to represent God with his whole being and to represent his community with his whole being. Yet the complex representational responsibilities of the prophet and their dynamic interaction do not end there, because the one who is called to perform these prophetic representational tasks does not, for that reason, cease to be an individual with a distinct personality and particular concerns. Although it may seem obvious, we must not neglect the fact that the prophet continues to represent himself while also performing his tasks of representing God and his community.

A PROPHET REPRESENTS HIMSELF

Among the interconnected web of prophetic responsibilities described and executed within the biblical texts we find passages in which the prophets' own concerns predominate. Of course, the prophet, as any individual, represents himself verbally, behaviorally, and affectively. Although these three aspects cannot be absolutely separated, we will consider passages that show the prophets engaged in personal concerns primarily of one sort or another.

Verbally

We can never strictly isolate the prophets' verbal communication from their other representational functions inasmuch as we're ultimately dealing with a text—a collection of words. But at times the focus of these words is largely on the prophet himself rather than on God or the community.

When Isaiah, for example, receives his vision of the sovereign Lord seated on his heavenly throne and receiving praise from seraphs (Isa. 6:1–4), it is a revelation that Isaiah alone experiences. His divine call and commissioning as a prophet of the Lord (Isa. 6:5–13), as well as the divine call and commissioning of all of the prophets, are directed first and foremost to the prophet as an individual.[18] Isaiah's response to his vision of the divine has, therefore, primary significance for him alone: "Woe to me! . . . I am ruined! For I am a man of unclean lips, and I live among a people of unclean lips, and my eyes have seen the King, the LORD Almighty" (v. 5).

When Amos defends himself against the verbal attacks of Amaziah, the priest of Bethel (Amos 7:14), it is difficult to see by his words a representation of anything other than his own situation: "I was neither a prophet nor a prophet's son, but I was a shepherd, and I also took care of sycamore-fig trees."

Similarly, within the context of his representational pre-enactment of the siege of Judah by performing certain be-

---

18. Even in this apparently individualistic experience, however, as well as in those that follow, there is an element of representation involved, inasmuch as Israel (and the church) also receives a divine call and commission.

haviors that would characterize that time (Ezek. 4:14), Ezekiel manifests his own personal indignation at the Lord's command for him to demonstrate the coming shortage of cooking fuel by using human excrement to bake his food: "Not so, Sovereign LORD! I have never defiled myself. From my youth until now I have never eaten anything found dead or torn by wild animals. No unclean meat has ever entered my mouth."

Jeremiah comments on the refreshing nature of his dream-filled sleep in words that refer to an experience all his own: "At this I awoke and looked around. My sleep had been pleasant to me" (Jer. 31:26).

These and the many other similar examples that could be adduced are sufficient to establish the obvious, yet often overlooked, conclusion that the prophets' words often are directed toward their own concerns as they represent themselves verbally.

Behaviorally

We also find passages within the prophetic writings that show us the prophets busy about their own affairs. Even though the prophets have the weighty responsibilities of representing God and their communities, they do not for that reason cease to be human beings who must attend to the concerns of everyday life. In passages that give us brief glimpses of the prophets tending to such affairs, we see the prophets as individuals just as unique as any of us, attending to the affairs of life that involve them.

Again, due to its length, the book of Jeremiah affords us with the most opportunities to see such personal behavior on the part of a prophet. We find Jeremiah, for example, traveling to and from the places where the Lord has sent him to prophesy (Jer. 19:14). During the periods between formal proclamations, the prophet was alone with his thoughts, temporarily relieved to a large degree (though never entirely) from his other representational responsibilities. We find Jeremiah being pressed by the crowd after his prophecy concerning the destruction of Jerusalem and the temple (Jer. 26:9). In another passage, we can practically see Jeremiah yawn and stretch as he reorients himself to his surroundings after a sleep filled with revelatory dreams (Jer. 31:26). We are given the details of Jeremiah's purchase of his cousin's field (Jer. 32:9–12). We see Jeremiah going about his personal business in Jeremiah 37:11–15, where we are told that "Jeremiah started to leave the city to go to the territory of Benjamin to get his share of the property among the people there."

These fleeting glimpses into the personal behaviors of the prophets remind us that these functionaries were real people who attended to the everyday affairs of life in addition to their important tasks of representing God and their community.

Affectively

As we would expect, these individuals demonstrate not only personal behaviors, but also personal affections. We must always be careful to consider the representative dimension of the affections about which the text informs us, but sometimes in the words recorded in Scripture we see displayed affections that are unique to, or at least primarily focusing upon, the prophet. These are evident in the course of the prophets' conversations with God or with others.

We find the prophets exhibiting various emotions, for example, when they receive their divine calls.[19] In other situations too we are occasionally given insight into the private emotions of the prophets. Consider the so-called confes-

19. See Isa. 6:1–13; Jer. 1:4–10.

sions of Jeremiah, passages that give us access to his inner-most struggles with his calling, his situation, and even his re-lationship with God (Jer. 11:18–23; 12:1–4; 15:10–21; 17:12–18; 18:18–23; 20:7–18). In the same way, Jonah's prayer in the belly of the great fish (Jonah 2) clearly and pri-marily lays bare the prophet's own spiritual struggles and mental anguish, in addition to any wider representative character it may possess. While we can never discount a rep-resentative aspect to any of the prophet's words, behaviors, or affections, at times the emphasis seems to be on the prophet himself.

A PROPHET'S REPRESENTATIVE FUNCTIONS INTERWEAVE

We have already stated that it is almost impossible for the verbal, behavioral, and affective aspects of the prophets' representative functions to be separated from one another in actual experience. What is true for each representative func-tion is true for the functions as a whole. That is, a prophet never entirely ceases to represent God, his community, and himself, and he never entirely ceases to do this verbally, be-haviorally, and affectively. All of these dimensions are pres-ent to some degree at all times. It couldn't be otherwise. A prophet does not consciously decide to stop representing God with his whole being for a period of time during which he will then start representing his community, again with his whole being. Nor does a prophet decide that he will stop al-lowing his own personality to exist. These aspects of a prophet's life coexist and intermingle in a complex, dynamic interaction throughout his entire ministry.

Consider the similar case of a pastor today. When he comes before the congregation to deliver God's word, he consciously bears the important responsibility of representing God to his covenant people. Yet the pastor does not for that reason cease to be a member of the congregation to which he is delivering that word. Thus he can also effectively represent the people of God by his congregational prayers and by exhibiting in himself the concerns shared by the larger community. Nevertheless, he also has his own personal anxieties, fears, goals, ambitions, joys, preferences, and interests that vie for his attention and manifest themselves in his words, behaviors, and affections. Which of these functions—representing God, the congregation, or himself—is at the forefront of his mind at any given time depends to a large extent upon the specific task in which he is engaged, but he is never entirely uninfluenced by any of them.

We may find one, two, or more of these representative functions of the prophet to be readily discernible in any prophetic passage we examine. In fact, these different representative functions of the prophet can be so intertwined that it is sometimes difficult to determine in what capacity the prophet is primarily functioning. Let's consider a few examples.

In Isaiah's long song of praise in chapter 26:7–21, note how many times the speaker changes. In verses 7–8, that Isaiah is representing his community is evident by his use of the words "we" and "our" in his address to God. Isaiah is including himself in the larger community of God's people, whose concerns he brings to the Lord. In the very next verses, however (vv. 9–11), Isaiah speaks in the singular first person, as evidenced by the phrase "my soul" in verse 9. He once again includes himself with the community in verses 12–15, using the word "us" repeatedly. Then, in verse 16, the prophet separates himself from the community once again by using the pronouns "they" and "them" to refer to his own people. Immediately after this verse, however, he rejoins the community by his repeated use of the pronoun "we" (vv.

17–18). The speaker is hard to determine in verse 19. Here Isaiah could very well be representing God directly by proclaiming a future resurrection. Verse 20 seems to shift in the middle from an exhortation by God to a statement from the prophet. This is demonstrated by the words "my people," apparently spoken by God to his people, followed immediately by a reference to God in the third person ("his wrath") that continues into the next verse.

We may also observe a shift in the prophet's representational functions in Jeremiah 4:22–26. This passage begins with the prophet speaking in the first person, for God: "My people are fools; they do not know me." It ends with the prophet speaking in the third person, about God: "All its towns lay in ruins before the LORD, before his fierce anger."

We can see after a consideration of only these two passages, out of many like them, how complicated is the interplay of the representative functions of a prophet. The shift from first to second to third person in prophetic passages is largely the result of this complex psychological, multirepresentational prophetic responsibility manifesting itself in the text, and not, as some scholars have suggested, the result of a capricious and clumsy patching together of unrelated texts by a later, inept editor.[20]

To understand the interplay of the prophets' representational functions on a larger level, consider the entire book of Jonah. Surely Jonah's resentment of the Lord's gracious offer to spare the Ninevites—that dreaded and despised enemy of Israel—if they repented, was a deeply personal

---

20. For the difficulties of maintaining the critical hypothesis of "accepted" source distinctions in the book of Jeremiah, for example, even if we accept the critical criteria, see Michael J. Williams, "An Investigation of the Legitimacy of Source Distinctions for the Prose Material in Jeremiah," *JBL* 112/2 (1993): 193–210.

emotion of Jonah's. There is no doubt that we are reading his very own feelings on the matter. Yet Jonah's feelings certainly characterized the sentiments of the entire community of God's people whom he represented. The Lord's patient dealings with Jonah in order to bring him to the point where he would carry out the task he was called to do (that is, communicate God's salvation to the world) reflects God's similar purpose in dealing with Israel. Finally, when Jonah at last engages in the task he was sent to perform, his call for repentance is understood by the Ninevites to be the very word of God.[21] So we see how difficult a question it is when we ask whom Jonah is representing in the book that bears his name. In our efforts to answer this question we come face to face with the overlapping and simultaneous representative tasks of the prophet.

That prophetic communication is so multidimensional should not surprise us, for this is what the church has confessed concerning Scripture for millennia.[22] The Bible is the Word of God. In revealing his will to us in this special revelation, however, God did not override the personalities of the human authors, nor did he remove them from their communities or from a responsibility to attend to or display their own concerns. Rather, God uses all of these aspects of the prophet's life, what we have been calling his representative functions, to communicate the divine will in a variety of ways and at a variety of levels. We are only beginning to become accustomed to "hearing" this commu-

---

21. In Jonah 3:5 we are told, "The Ninevites believed God." They obviously understood that Jonah's words were not issued on his own authority, but rather on the authority of God himself.

22. For a survey of the church's appreciation for and wrestling with the multidimensional character of prophetic communication, see the excellent discussion by John Breck, *The Power of the Word: In the Worshipping Church* (Crestwood, N.Y.: St. Vladimir's Seminary, 1986), 35–92.

nication as it comes to us by way of avenues other than the
direct speech with which we are so familiar in our Western
culture. Yet, when we read, or reread, the prophetic texts
with sensitivity to these other ways of communication,
those texts become richer and their meaning is more fully
realized and appreciated. Not only do we begin to understand how God is using the prophets in the totality of their
beings to bring us to a comprehension of his will, but we
also begin to see possibilities for us to communicate his
truth to those around us in new, more diverse, and more
comprehensive ways.

Now that we have been introduced to the prophetic
function of representation in its different aspects, how
does this help us in our desire to apply those representative tasks to the church today? Before we answer this question, we must answer another one that it presupposes: Is it
possible for the kind of representation that characterizes
the prophetic office to be carried out by *a community?* Has
this ever been done before? If the church—a community in
the fullest sense of the term—is to function in a prophetic
capacity in the world today, these are essential questions.
Once again, we need look no further for an answer to our
questions than that wonderful body of divine revelation in
which God has communicated to us everything we need to
know in order to accomplish his will. There is, after all, a
rather large and extensive body of material in the Bible
that deals precisely with the questions we are asking. Preserved and transmitted to us in the Old Testament, in the
redemptive history of Israel, is the answer to whether or
not a community is able to carry out the prophetic functions. In the next chapter, we examine Israel from this
prophetic perspective in order to prepare ourselves for the
possibility and implications of a truly prophetic witness for
the church today.

FOR FURTHER REFLECTION

1. How does God make his word known to the prophet? How does he make his word known to us today?

2. Describe a recent experience in your own life in which your words, actions, and emotions were all working together to express your thoughts. Reflect on how the perception of your message would have been different if one of these aspects of your communication was out of synch with the others.

3. What parallels do you see between the prophet's various representational responsibilities and the responsibilities of a contemporary pastor?

4. How does a prophet's own individuality figure into his prophetic calling?

5. Reflect on how you communicate the truth of God to others. What areas of communication do you emphasize, and what areas might need improving?

THE PROPHETIC ROLE OF ISRAEL

Even though we may be sorely tempted to pass by a consideration of Israel on our biblical-theological highway toward application, such a move would merit the equivalent of an exegetical speeding ticket. Before we attempt such an interpretive effort, however, it is first necessary for us to establish whether the prophetic representative functions we have been considering could ever be broadened so as to be carried out legitimately and intentionally by a community rather than, or in addition to, an individual. Thankfully, this information has already been provided for us by the biblical accounts of Israel, the Old Testament community of God's people.

There is a vast amount of popular material available these days that purports to explain and promote the role of the church in the world. Sadly, however, relatively little of this material reflects back on the biblical accounts of God's covenant community of the past to see what God is teaching us today through the carefully selected and preserved materials of the Old Testament. It's as though we are wearing historical blinders that prevent us from looking backward in time to learn what we can from the rich experiences of those who have gone before us.

Instead of imposing upon ourselves such an unnecessary interpretive handicap, our goal in this chapter is to learn as much as we can from the enscripturated narratives of Israel's history. Our special focus will be on how the redemptive history of Israel may actually provide for us a model of a community carrying out the role of a prophet in the world. After all, Israel's entrance into and occupation of a foreign land, during which they interact in a host of ways with their ancient Near Eastern neighbors, can be regarded as nothing less than the covenant community engaging a hostile culture with the truth about God and humanity. Isn't this what the church is all about? Understanding the prophetic pattern behind Israel's life as a nation will enable us intelligently, carefully, and legitimately to apply that pattern to the church today as we seek our own engagement with an often hostile culture. We proceed, therefore, by considering each of the representational tasks of the prophet as they find expression in the life of the community of Israel.[1]

ISRAEL REPRESENTS GOD

Just as one of the tasks of a prophet involves communicating God's message to the community of which the prophet is a member, so also one of Israel's prophetic tasks involved communicating God's message to the community of which she was a member. But what community was that?

---

1. I use the term "Israel" loosely and conveniently to refer to God's covenant community in its various stages in the Old Testament. Thus the term is used to denote the exodus community, the twelve tribes, the united monarchy, the twin kingdoms of Israel and Judah, the remaining kingdom of Judah after Israel has been conquered, and even the remnant returning from exile.

There was, in fact, a community of which Israel was a member, for the simple reason that Israel was not a nation that existed in isolation from her ancient Near Eastern neighbors. She was subject to the same regional circumstances as they were. She was just one member of a larger *community of nations* with whom she interacted, engaging in commerce, forming military and economic partnerships, and conducting warfare. Thus the community to which Israel was responsible to communicate God's message was the community of nations in which she found herself. We may therefore correctly conclude that just as God communicated his message to the prophet, and the prophet in turn communicated that message to his community (Israel), so Israel was responsible to communicate that message to her community (the other nations). Graphically, this is illustrated in figure 1.

FIGURE 1
Israel Represents God

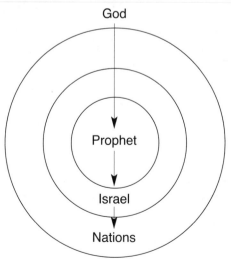

Remember that the individual prophet represents God to his community through his words and his experiences (his behaviors and affections). It was possible for Israel to accomplish this same task in the same ways by functioning as though she were essentially an individual, or a corporate personality. By corporate personality I mean a group, community, institution, or company that behaves as an individual.[2] In his discussion of how this concept of corporate personality manifests itself in relation to the nation of Israel, H. Wheeler Robinson argues that the Old Testament prophets viewed Israel's history, from its inception to the time in which they spoke, as an essential unity:

> The corporate personality of the family, clan, and the people was conceived realistically as a unity, a unity which made possible the all-important doctrine of election, and lent unity to the history itself. Amos can address his contemporaries in the eighth century as still "the whole family which I brought up out of the land of Egypt," since they are both its representatives and its actual constituents. The people *are* their ancestors, as the patriarchal narratives often illustrate. The conception of history as a unity derives in the last resort through Christianity from the Hebrew prophets and apocalyptists, and they are working with the unity of corporate personality.[3]

2. This idea of corporate personality stems from the legal concept of a corporation, defined by Bryan A. Garner, ed., *Black's Law Dictionary* (St. Paul: West Group, 1999), 341, as "a group or succession of persons established in accordance with legal rules into a legal or juristic person that has legal personality distinct from the natural persons who make it up, exists indefinitely apart from them, and has the legal powers that its constitution gives it."

3. H. Wheeler Robinson, *Corporate Personality in Ancient Israel*, 2d ed. (Edinburgh: T. & T. Clark, 1981), 29.

Not only do the prophets often view Israel as a corporate personality in the sense described, but Israel herself also behaves as a corporate personality when it comes to carrying out the prophetic functions, for which the biblical accounts give abundant evidence. We turn now, therefore, to a consideration of the biblical evidence that demonstrates how Israel fulfills her prophetic calling in all of its various aspects.

Verbally

The knowledge of the truth imparted to Israel by the Creator of all things was never meant to be hoarded by her, as though it were ever intended to be hers alone. From the very beginning of her existence as a nation she had the responsibility of transmitting this information to the surrounding nations.[4] Indeed, her deliverance from Egypt, her safe entry into the Promised Land, her protection from her enemies round about, and her providential care by the Lord of heaven and earth should have constrained her to proclaim his praise to every other nation. The psalmist encourages Israel to do precisely this in Psalm 96:2–3: "Sing to the LORD, praise his name; proclaim his salvation day after day. Declare his glory *among the nations,* his marvelous deeds *among all peoples.*"

There are times and occasions in Israel's history when she does, in fact, verbally testify about her God to the inhabitants of other nations. In his encounters with Pharaoh (Exod. 5–12), Moses calls the Lord "the God of Israel" (5:1), "the God of the Hebrews" who has met with them and demands their release so that he may receive their worship (5:3; 9:1, 13; 10:3). Moses, speaking for the Lord, clearly proclaims to Pharaoh the universal sovereignty of the true God:

---

4. David E. Holwerda, *Jesus and Israel: One Covenant or Two?* (Grand Rapids: Eerdmans, 1995), 57: "Israel's central calling was to be a light to the nations."

Let my people go, so that they may worship me, or
. . . I will send the full force of my plagues against
you and against your officials and your people, *so you
may know that there is no one like me in all the earth.*
For by now I could have stretched out my hand and
struck you and your people with a plague that would
have wiped you off the earth. But I have raised you
up for this very purpose, that I might show you my
power *and that my name might be proclaimed in all the
earth.* (Exod. 9:13–16)

Much later, in his confrontation with Goliath, the Philistine champion, the young boy David also testifies to God's
power, and his intention to give his people victory:

You come against me with sword and spear and
javelin, but I come against you in the name of the
LORD Almighty, the God of the armies of Israel,
whom you have defied. This day the LORD will hand
you over to me . . . *and the whole world will know that
there is a God in Israel.* All those gathered here will
know that it is not by sword or spear that the LORD
saves; for the battle is the LORD's, and he will give all
of you into our hands. (1 Sam. 17:45–47)

After many years, David's son Solomon writes a letter to
Hiram, the king of Tyre, in which he too testifies to the providential care of the God of Israel:

You know that because of the wars waged against my
father David from all sides, he could not build a temple for the Name of the LORD his God until the
LORD put his enemies under his feet. But now the
LORD my God has given me rest on every side, and

there is no adversary or disaster. I intend, therefore, to build a temple for the Name of the LORD my God, as the LORD told my father David, when he said, "Your son whom I will put on the throne in your place will build a temple for my Name." So give orders that cedars of Lebanon be cut for me. (1 Kings 5:3–6)

These examples, and others that could be added to them, indicate that there were those within Israel who, at least occasionally, communicated the truth about their God to those outside the covenant community. Yet these examples are not as frequent as we would perhaps expect. It appears that Israel very often failed to undertake willingly this prophetic task of representing God with words. She had been singled out from all the nations to be "a light for the Gentiles" (Isa. 42:6), to bring God's salvation to the ends of the earth (that is, to all of the other nations on earth; Isa. 49:6) by pointing the way toward the giver of life. Nevertheless, she herself is forced to confess that she had not "brought salvation to the earth" (Isa. 26:18). However, Israel would be a light to the Gentiles even in spite of herself (Isa. 51:4). God's purposes cannot be hindered by disobedience, and God's prophetic purpose for Israel could in no way be thwarted by her disobedience. This truth is illustrated by the book of Jonah. As *The NIV Study Bible* correctly notes:

The author [of the book of Jonah] uses the art of representative roles in a straightforward manner. In this story of God's loving concern for all people, Nineveh, the great menace to Israel, is representative of the Gentiles. Correspondingly, stubbornly reluctant Jonah represents Israel's jealousy of her favored relationship with God and her unwillingness to share the Lord's compassion with the nations.[5]

Like Jonah, Israel had refused her prophetic calling to proclaim the salvation of God to the Gentiles. Also like Jonah, Israel would nevertheless end up proclaiming that salvation in spite of herself. How she actually does this leads us to the consideration of another avenue by which a prophet represents God to his community.

Experientially

Earlier we saw that in addition to representing God to his community verbally, a prophet also does so behaviorally and affectively. Because the affective representation of God by a nation is a little hard to quantify, we will combine these two aspects into the more general category of experience. How did Israel's *experience* as a nation convey the message God intended to communicate to the community of nations of which she was a member?

God's dealings with Israel were always intended to communicate his attributes, such as his power, righteousness, and holiness, to the witnessing nations round about. Joshua, for example, explains to the Israelites, after they had crossed the Jordan and entered into the land of promise, that this demonstration of God's power (and the earlier demonstration at the Red Sea) was intended as a public testimony for all the peoples of the earth:

> The LORD your God dried up the Jordan before you until you had crossed over. The LORD your God did

---

5. Kenneth Barker, ed., *The NIV Study Bible: New International Version* (Grand Rapids: Zondervan, 1985), 1364. For a minority dissenting view, see R. E. Clements, "The Purpose of the Book of Jonah," VTSup 28 (1974): 16–28.

to the Jordan just what he had done to the Red Sea
when he dried it up before us until we had crossed
over. He did this *so that all the peoples of the earth
might know* that the hand of the LORD is powerful
and so that you might always fear the LORD your
God. (Josh. 4:23–24)

Through his gracious and active involvement in the
life of his chosen people and his efforts on their behalf
God gains for himself everlasting renown not only among
them, but also throughout the whole world (Isa.
63:12–14). In his prayer, Nehemiah recounts how the
miraculous signs and wonders God sent against Pharaoh,
his officials, and all Egypt "made a name" for himself,
"which remains to this day" (Neh. 9:10). God's deliverance of his people from their bondage in Egypt and from
the mighty Egyptian army that was pursuing them after
their departure communicated loudly and clearly to all
who witnessed it the power and glory of Israel's God—a
communication that did not require words for it to be
comprehended.

We need not be in any doubt about whether this message
was, in fact, received by the surrounding nations. The nations' appreciation for the significance of the exodus events
was anticipated by Moses and the Israelites after the Lord
had led them through the Red Sea and is reflected in their
victory song: "The nations will hear and tremble; anguish
will grip the people of Philistia. The chiefs of Edom will be
terrified, the leaders of Moab will be seized with trembling,
the people of Canaan will melt away; terror and dread will
fall upon them" (Exod. 15:14–16). Later, when Joshua
sends spies to reconnoiter the Promised Land, Rahab reports to them that the nations had indeed received the message concerning Israel's God:

> We have heard how the LORD dried up the water of
> the Red Sea for you when you came out of Egypt,
> and what you did to Sihon and Og, the two kings of
> the Amorites east of the Jordan, whom you com-
> pletely destroyed. When we heard of it, our hearts
> melted and everyone's courage failed because of you,
> for the LORD your God is God in heaven above and
> on the earth below. (Josh. 2:10–11)

In these passages we read of foreign nations *hearing*
about God's miraculous exercise of power on behalf of his
people. This may cause some confusion in a section where
we are talking not about verbal communication, but about
visible communication, dramatic actions. Keep in mind,
however, that the content of the reports the foreign nations
are hearing is not propositional truth about Israel's God that
the Israelites, obedient to their prophetic calling to verbally
represent God, are communicating. Rather, what the nations hear comes by way of intermediaries and consists of reports about what Israel's God *has done*. These are reports
about actions, and the reports themselves testify that the actions have theological significance that is recognized by
those who are doing the reporting. A similar testimony to
the effectiveness of this type of nonverbal communication is
later provided in Joshua 5:1: "When all the Amorite kings
west of the Jordan and all the Canaanite kings along the
coast heard how the LORD had dried up the Jordan before
the Israelites . . . their hearts melted and they no longer had
the courage to face the Israelites."

Not only in his militaristic intervention on their behalf,
but also in his more general, providential care for his people,
God communicates truths about himself. Thus the psalmist
prays that other nations may learn about God as a result of
his care for his people (Ps. 67:1–2): "May God be gracious

to us and bless us and make his face shine upon us, *that your ways may be known on earth, your salvation among all nations.*" God also shows his attributes of holiness and justice when he punishes his people for their rejection of him:

> Therefore my people will go into exile
>   for lack of understanding;
> their men of rank will die of hunger
>   and their masses will be parched with thirst.
> . . . .
> So man will be brought low
>   and mankind humbled,
>   the eyes of the arrogant humbled.
> But the LORD Almighty will be exalted by his justice,
>   and the holy God will *show himself* holy by his
>   righteousness. (Isa. 5:13–16)

When God delivers his people from their exile, his gracious intervention not only benefits Israel, but also manifests his holiness, mercy, and compassion "in the sight of the nations": "This is what the Sovereign LORD says: When I gather the people of Israel from the nations where they have been scattered, I will *show myself* holy among them *in the sight of the nations*" (Ezek. 28:25).

From the very beginning of her existence, Israel always had the responsibility to engage actively in her task of being "a light for the Gentiles" (Isa. 42:6; 49:6). She was to communicate clearly the truth about her God not only with words, but also with her behavior. It would benefit us to take a moment to consider this target audience in more detail if we are to determine whether Israel's communication to them was indeed effective. Who are these "Gentiles" to whom Israel was supposed to communicate? They certainly included the nations surrounding Israel in her historical, ancient Near Eastern existence. However, we need to broaden our perspective to include much more than this. We are repeatedly told, in fact, that Israel's witness was to go far beyond the localized community of nations that inhabited her particular part of the planet and extend to "all peoples" or "all nations" (e.g., Ps. 96:2–3; Isa. 26:17–18; 42:6; 49:6). Israel's witness was not to be limited geographically.

However, even this is not a sufficiently broad perspective. We must also recognize that the target audience of Israel's witness is not to be limited chronologically either. That is, by means of his interaction with Israel, God has effectively communicated his redemptive revelation to the nations *throughout time*. He has accomplished this remarkable (and seldom considered) feat by recording in Scripture those aspects of Israel's national experience that communicate the truths about him that he wills the nations to know, and then providentially preserving these words throughout time (Ps. 119:89; Isa. 40:8; Matt. 5:18; 24:35). Every time we pick up the Bible and read the Old Testament accounts of God's dealings with his chosen people, Israel once again fulfills her calling of being a light, or prophetic witness of divine truth, to the Gentiles.

We have seen that a prophet does not just represent God, but also represents the larger community of which he is a member. If Israel really does perform the prophetic function completely, therefore, she must also, at least in some fashion, represent the community of nations of which she is a member.

ISRAEL REPRESENTS THE NATIONS

Israel's prophetic function of representing the community of nations is illustrated graphically in figure 2. The diagram is intended to illustrate that just as the nation of Israel could look toward the prophet to see a miniature represen-

FIGURE 2
Israel Represents the Nations

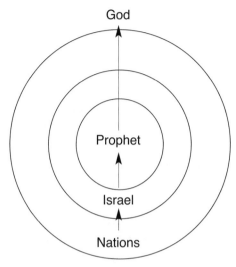

tation of herself and learn about her own future from what God was doing with the prophet, so the nations could look toward Israel to see a picture of themselves and also learn what God was going to be doing with them. Remember that the individual prophet represents his community by means of his words and his experiences (his behaviors and affections). Israel accomplishes this same task for the nations in the same ways. Let's take a closer look at how Old Testament Israel, as a corporate personality, continues to fulfill this prophetic calling by representing the nations verbally and experientially.

Verbally

How does the nation of Israel represent the Gentile nations with words? We have seen that the individual prophet represents his community verbally by means of intercessory prayer. There are also several instances in Scripture where Israelites intercede for non-Israelites.

Abraham's deception had led Abimelech to end up in an extremely compromising situation with Sarah, Abraham's wife. Abimelech was kept from sin by God and instructed by him in a dream to "return the man's wife, for he is a prophet, and he will pray for you and you will live" (Gen. 20:7). We must not pass too quickly over this remarkable passage without noting a couple of very important points. First, we note that Abraham is praying for someone who is outside the community of God's people. Second, we note that this passage contains the first mention of the word "prophet" in the Bible. If one did not bring any preconceptions to the text and encountered this word here for the first time, one would conclude that an essential function of a prophet is to pray for others—and one would, in fact, be correct.

In chapters 8–9 of the book of Exodus, after receiving (false) promises of release from Pharaoh, Moses repeatedly prays to God on behalf of Pharaoh and the Egyptians that the plagues they were suffering would be removed. Even though Pharaoh's promises were insincere, Moses' prayers for him and his people were answered in each case.

There is yet another way in which Israel represents the nations with words. Israel was meant to be an example, a visual picture, of what God intended for all nations. Thus Israel's communication with God using words pictured the communication God intended between himself and all nations. That is, the prayer of Israel, in addition to being genuine communication between her and God, was also intended to be a foreshadowing or preview of the communication between all nations and God that was possible in Old Testament times, but that would be secured and engendered through the mediator of the New Covenant, Jesus Christ. This representational dimension of Israel's prayer is explicated in a couple important passages of the Old Testament.

The first of these is found, appropriately, within

Solomon's prayer at the dedication of the newly constructed temple. In the midst of his requests that God would answer his people when they pray toward the temple, Solomon inserts a request that the prayers of foreigners would also be answered:

> As for the foreigner who does not belong to your people Israel but has come from a distant land because of your name—for men will hear of your great name and your mighty hand and your outstretched arm—when he comes and prays toward this temple, then hear from heaven, your dwelling place, and do whatever the foreigner asks of you, *so that all the peoples of the earth may know your name and fear you, as do your own people Israel,* and may know that this house I have built bears your Name. (1 Kings 8:41–43)

Solomon's prayer recognizes that Israel occupies a representative place in God's redemptive plan, a plan that ultimately involves "all the peoples of the earth." Israel's prayer, therefore, ultimately represents prayer that would be uttered by foreigners, too.

In Isaiah 56:6–7, Isaiah prophesies that there will be a day when those who have been excluded from formal worship in Israel, including foreigners, would be welcomed into God's house of prayer. Isaiah highlights the representational aspect of Israel's prayer by noting that the house that was the focal point of prayer in Israel, the temple, would then be called "a house of prayer for all nations":

> And foreigners who bind themselves to the LORD
>   to serve him,
>   to love the name of the LORD,
>   and to worship him,

all who keep the Sabbath without desecrating it
  and who hold fast to my covenant—
these I will bring to my holy mountain
  and give them joy in my house of prayer.
Their burnt offerings and sacrifices
  will be accepted on my altar;
for my house will be called
  a house of prayer for all nations.

While we have seen that Israel's words point toward greater realities in the future, the representational character of Israel's existence—indeed, its divinely appointed prophetic task—extends beyond words. The entirety of Israel's experiences contributes to their prophetic message, and by means of these experiences they more comprehensively fulfill their responsibility to represent the nations.

Experientially

The experiential aspect of Israel's prophetic function is perhaps the most intriguing to think about for the simple reason that it is so rarely considered. When we give this dimension of Israel's prophetic character a closer look, the richness and cohesiveness of the entire Old Testament suddenly become much more apparent, and we are consequently able to comprehend in a new way the message that God is communicating through the history of his interaction with his chosen people. As we grow more accustomed to reading the historical accounts of Israel with an eye for their prophetic implications, our reading of the Old Testament will slow and become more fruitful as its contemporary relevance becomes obvious. For just as what the individual prophet experienced has revelatory significance and points toward what the nation as a whole would experience, so the experiences of Israel preserved for us in the Old Testament are not just random accounts of unrelated events, but have significance and point toward what God was intending to do for all of the nations through his Son. These are large statements and require some justification before we proceed.

The apostle Paul explains that "everything that was written in the past was written to teach us, so that through endurance and the encouragement of the Scriptures we might have hope" (Rom. 15:4). The "us" he refers to here unquestionably includes the members of the church at Rome to which he was writing. These recipients of Paul's letter were predominantly Gentile believers. We may therefore interpret Paul's statement to say that everything written in the Scriptures (which at the time of his writing meant the body of literature comprising our current Old Testament), all of the materials concerning national Israel included in the Bible, were meant to be instructive even for Gentile believers far removed from the time period during which those events occurred. Details about Israel's national experience, therefore, have a continuing significance for Gentiles. That is, Israel continues to be a prophetic witness to the nations (including us) by means of what is recorded about her in Scripture.

Later, in his first letter to the church at Corinth, Paul explicitly states that the events of Israel's national experience have typological significance for the church today. That is, just as the behavior of the individual prophet could communicate truth about God to Israel, so the behavior, the events, the experiences of national Israel communicate truth about God to the larger world.[6] Discussing Israel's exodus from

---

6. Hans K. LaRondelle, *The Israel of God in Prophecy: Principles of Prophetic Interpretation* (Berrien Springs, Mich.: Andrews University Press, 1983), 17: "Promises concerning Israel as a people, dynasty, land, city, and mountain are not self-contained, isolated promises for the sake of Israel, but are integral parts of God's progressive plan of salvation for the world and the human race."

Egypt, their divine leading and provision, and their subsequent judgment as well, Paul states, "These things occurred as examples to keep us from setting our hearts on evil things as they did" (1 Cor. 10:6). Following a description of several specific instances of Israel's disobedience and consequent punishment, Paul again states, "These things happened to them as examples and were written down as warnings for us, on whom the fulfillment of the ages has come" (1 Cor. 10:11). The word translated as "examples" in 1 Corinthians 10:6, 11 is the Greek word τύποι (*typoi,* from the root τύπος, or *typos*) from which we get our English word "type." In other words, these experiences of Israel are types from which we are supposed to learn.

TYPOLOGY VERSUS ALLEGORY

Before we proceed to a consideration of some of these typological experiences of Israel and their implications for us today, we need to review briefly what we mean by types and typological interpretation. A biblical type has been defined as "a fact or incident of history . . . of exalted dignity and worth—one divinely ordained by the omniscient Ruler to be a foreshadowing of the good things which he purposed in the fullness of time to bring to pass through the mediation of Jesus Christ."[7] Typological interpretation is, therefore, a method of understanding the biblical text that seeks to determine the significance of the types of the Old Testament in light of their redemptive fulfillment in Christ. For example, the sacrifices of the Old Testament are universally understood to be types of the ultimate self-sacrifice of Jesus Christ. This is the testimony of Scripture itself (Heb. 9–10).

---

7. Milton S. Terry, *Biblical Hermeneutics: A Treatise on the Interpretation of the Old and New Testaments* (Grand Rapids: Zondervan, 1974), 336.

In matters of this sort we are on safe ground and are introducing nothing new. However, we must at this point leave the well-trodden path, break out our exegetical machetes, and forge ahead into less-explored territory.

We have seen that a prophet communicates by his experiences what his community as a whole will experience. For example, the imprisonment of Jeremiah was a type of the Babylonian captivity of the nation as a whole. Those in the nation of Judah who witnessed Jeremiah's arrest and incarceration at the hands of King Zedekiah could be certain that they had received a clear, though nonverbal, message concerning their own future. We have also seen that the demarcation or dividing lines between the prophetic functions (that is, representing God, representing the community of which the prophet is a member, and representing himself) are not easily drawn. We have considered instances in the prophetic texts where the precise representative function being exercised by the prophet at a given time is unclear. Certainly the prophet never ceases to perform all of his representative functions. There are times when one or more of these functions may receive greater emphasis than others, but all are active to some degree all the time. The same interplay between the prophetic representative functions is manifest in the enscripturated experiences of the nation of Israel. She certainly represents herself and her own national concerns, but she also—as we will see—and even at the same time, typologically represents by her experiences what God intends for all nations to experience. Therefore, in our reading of the Old Testament narratives of Israel's experiences, we must not limit our exegesis to only one of her representative functions while ignoring the rest. This would be turning a blind eye to prophetic communication that God intends for us to receive.

When we turn from interpretation of the biblical text to

a consideration of our own actual experience, we find that
we have no difficulty in comprehending how all of these representative functions can indeed be occurring at the same
time. Consider, for example, how these prophetic functions
interweave in the life of a contemporary pastor. As he speaks
God's word (representing God), he continues to be a member of his own congregation and shares their concerns, joys,
hurts, and happinesses (representing his community). At the
same time he continues to be an individual, of course, with
his own struggles, abilities, and contentments. We have considered the different aspects of the prophetic task separately
in the objective analysis we are undertaking here, but to keep
them separate in subjective, actual, day-to-day experience is
an impossibility. So, we must ask ourselves, is it legitimate to
maintain that there are times or experiences in the life of national Israel when she represents *only* what the nations were
to experience in God's redemptive program, and other times
when she completely ceases to perform this particular
prophetic function? Or, to put it another way, are there times
in Israel's national experience when she was a type and other
times when she was not?

Surprisingly, this question is usually answered in the af-
firmative by those who wish to restrict typological interpretation to discrete people, places, institutions, or events in the
life of Israel.[8] The apparent motivation for this limitation is
a fear of straying from the well-marked trail of acceptable
exegetical practice and wandering into that most dreaded

8. For example, Berkhof, *Principles of Biblical Interpretation*, 144–45; Leonhard
Goppelt, *Typos: The Typological Interpretation of the Old Testament in the New* (Grand
Rapids: Eerdmans, 1982), 17–18; Walter C. Kaiser and Moisés Silva, *An Introduction to Biblical Hermeneutics: The Search for Meaning* (Grand Rapids: Zondervan,
1994), 286; Terry, *Biblical Hermeneutics*, 336; and Anthony C. Thiselton, *New Horizons in Hermeneutics: The Theory and Practice of Transforming Biblical Reading* (Grand
Rapids: Zondervan, 1992), 155, 163.

and anathematized area of biblical interpretation: the allegorical method. The allegorical method of interpreting biblical texts has been described unflatteringly as "largely arbitrary, because the approved interpretation depended so largely on the interpreter's personal preference, and in practice it violated the original intention of the Scriptures and almost obliterated the historical relatedness of the revelation they recorded."[9] But the typological method of interpretation differs from this contemporary understanding[10] of the allegorical method in that it operates exclusively within the realm of actual redemptive history, while for allegory (it is charged) history of any sort is entirely unnecessary. In his exhaustive work on typology, Patrick Fairbairn summarizes this difference between typological (or typical) and allegorical interpretation:

> Typical interpretations of Scripture differ from allegorical ones . . . in that they indispensably require the reality of the facts or circumstances stated in the original narrative. And they differ also . . . in requiring . . . that the same truth or principle be embodied alike in the type and the antitype. *The typical is not properly a different or higher sense, but a different or higher application of the same sense.*[11]

9. F. F. Bruce, "Interpretation of the Bible," *EDT,* 566. For a description of the allegorical method, some historical reasons for its use, as well as some of its early practitioners, see Greidanus, *Preaching Christ from the Old Testament,* 70–89.

10. We must make a distinction here between the contemporary understanding of the allegorical method and how this method was actually historically understood and implemented by the Church Fathers. For example, Thomas Aquinas describes the "allegorical sense" in terms that we would readily accept if it were instead called the "typological sense": "So far as the things of the Old Law signify the things of the New Law, there is the allegorical sense" (*Summa Theologica,* part 1, question 1, article 10). The negative reaction of contemporary exegetes is often against a caricature of the allegorical method.

11. Patrick Fairbairn, *The Typology of Scripture* (Grand Rapids: Baker, 1975), 1:2–3.

Typological interpretation acknowledges and proceeds on the basis of the literal meaning of Scripture, while looking forward in time toward the redemptive realization of that literal meaning in the messianic age.[12] It is usually further safeguarded from the feared hermeneutical misstep into allegorical interpretation by assigning criteria for determining allowable types. These criteria include: (1) there must be a recognizable correspondence between the type and its antitype;[13] (2) the type and antitype must share the same fundamental reality and simply be historically separate expressions of it; and (3) the reality expressed by the type must find fuller expression in the antitype.[14]

Even under these strictures, the experiences of Israel recorded in Scripture, *taken as a whole*,[15] may be considered a type of God's coming redemptive activity with humankind on a broader level. To put it more simply, all of Israel's recorded experiences are prophetic of God's redemptive activity involving the human race. This, of course, presumes

12. Breck, *The Power of the Word*, 74–76; and Greidanus, *Preaching Christ from the Old Testament*, 91–92.

13. "Antitype" is the term used to signify the later realization in redemptive history of that toward which, it is argued, the type is pointing.

14. Breck, *The Power of the Word*, 82; Goppelt, *Typos*, 12–19, 224; Fairbairn, *The Typology of Scripture*, 1:42–51; and Terry, *Biblical Hermeneutics*, 337.

15. This is contrary to the usual assertion that types include only isolated events, persons, or institutions and not an entire collection thereof such as comprise the biblical account of Israel. For the restrictive view see, for example, Goppelt, *Typos*, 17–18; Terry, *Biblical Hermeneutics*, 336–37; and Berkhof, *Principles of Biblical Interpretation*, 144–45. For a discussion on the prophetic character of types, see Greidanus, *Preaching Christ from the Old Testament*, 250–52. Against this restrictive interpretation of types, see Tremper Longman III, *Immanuel in Our Place: Seeing Christ in Israel's Worship* (Phillipsburg, N.J.: P&R, 2001), viii: "Jesus did not arrive unannounced; his coming was declared *in advance* in the Old Testament, not just in explicit prophecies of the Messiah but by means of the stories of all of the events, characters, and circumstances in the Old Testament. . . . From the account of creation in Genesis to the final stories of the return from exile, God progressively unfolded his plan of salvation."

that types are prophetic and that Israel's experiences, not only considered individually but also considered in their entirety, are typical. John Goldingay's fear that understanding the Old Testament as a whole in this typological way "turn[s] real people or events that had significance of their own into mere representative symbols or puppets in a cosmic drama"[16] can easily be assuaged with the simple reminder that the prophetic task of representing through experiences the community of which the prophet is a member (which task is carried out on a large scale by Israel for humankind) is but one of the prophetic tasks. The prophet, considered as an individual or as a corporate personality, does not lose his individuality; that is, the prophet does not stop representing himself when he fulfills other representative functions.

It may well be argued that a greater danger than misuse of types is their neglect. Patrick Fairbairn gives us all fair warning of the terrible loss that results when biblical interpretation fails to give adequate attention to types:

> Were men accustomed, as they should be, to search for the germs of Christian truth in the earliest Scriptures, and to regard the inspired records of both covenants as having for their leading object "the testimony of Jesus," they would know how much they were losers by such an undue contraction of the typical element in Old Testament Scripture. And in proportion as a more profound and spiritual acquaintance with the divine word is cultivated, will the feeling of dissatisfaction grow in respect to a style of interpretation that so miserably dwarfs and crip-

16. John Goldingay, *Models for Interpretation of Scripture* (Grand Rapids: Eerdmans, 1995), 65.

ples the relation which the preparatory bears to the ultimate in God's revelation.[17]

Our fear of repeating past excesses (or introducing new ones) in typological interpretation should not cause us to commit the far graver error of abandoning this fruitful and divinely intentioned mode of communication.

EXAMPLES FROM ISRAEL'S HISTORY

Now that we have taken some time to reflect abstractly on the typological and prophetic character of Israel as recorded in Scripture, let's reflect on how Israel's national experience actually does point forward to (or represent, or typify) what God was going to do redemptively for all humanity through the person and work of Jesus Christ. While a review of the entire history of Israel from a typological perspective would exceed the bounds and needs of this book, we may at least examine briefly some of the defining experiences of God's covenant people in the Old Testament to understand how these events typify New Covenant realities.

Israel's national origins can be traced back to the call of Abraham in the opening verses of Genesis 12: "I will make you into a great nation and I will bless you; I will make your name great, and you will be a blessing. I will bless those who bless you, and whoever curses you I will curse; and all peoples on earth will be blessed through you." Abraham was appointed to be the one through whom God would build his chosen nation. To be an Israelite, therefore, is to be a descendant of Abraham (Matt. 3:9; Luke 3:8; John 8:39). This points forward to another community that would trace its ancestry back to one who is in a special relationship with

---

17. Fairbairn, *The Typology of Scripture*, 1:20.

God, Jesus Christ, through whom God is building a holy nation not restricted to geographical or ethnic boundaries. To be a Christian, therefore, is to be an adopted child of God through Jesus Christ: "In love he predestined us to be adopted as his sons through Jesus Christ" (Eph. 1:5). Patrick Fairbairn correctly concludes: "The natural Israel, then, as God's chosen people from among the peoples of the earth, were types of the elect seed, the spiritual and royal priesthood, whom Christ was to choose out of the world, and redeem for His everlasting kingdom."[18]

The nation of Israel proper was formed into a coherent community by the redemptive work of God. God redeemed his people from Egypt and delivered to them a national charter at Mount Sinai, which gave them a distinct identity as his separate, holy people. This historical reality points forward to a new community, a new nation, that God establishes through his redemptive work in Jesus Christ: "You are a chosen people, a royal priesthood, *a holy nation,* a people belonging to God, that you may declare the praises of him who called you out of darkness into his wonderful light" (1 Peter 2:9). Note that these are the same words spoken to the Israelites at Mount Sinai: "Although the whole earth is mine, you will be for me a kingdom of priests and a holy nation" (Exod. 19:5–6).

Israel was delivered from slavery to Pharaoh in Egypt, and Christians are delivered from a bondage even more oppressive and penetrating—slavery to sin (Rom. 6:20–23). Indeed, the typology of the exodus is universally maintained in patristic exegesis and confirmed by the New Testament.

> The Fathers have rightly insisted at all times that the types of the Exodus are fulfilled in the life of Christ

---

18. Fairbairn, *The Typology of Scripture,* 1:416.

and the Church, and in this they have but followed the teaching of the New Testament, which shows that these types are fulfilled in Christ. But the New Testament is itself only the continuation of the Old, and never fails to emphasize that the New Exodus foretold in the Old Testament has been realized in Jesus Christ of Nazareth.[19]

Israel was provided manna in the desert to sustain them during the forty years of wandering. From this they learned to depend on God for their physical nourishment. The apostle John records for us Christ's own typological interpretation of this historical reality: "Your forefathers ate the manna in the desert, yet they died. But here is the bread that comes down from heaven, which a man may eat and not die. I am the living bread that came down from heaven. If anyone eats of this bread, he will live forever. This bread is my flesh, which I will give for the life of the world" (John 6:49–51). Here we have, once again, a scriptural example of an actual experience of Israel that is laden with prophetic relevance. In the context of his general statement that the events of Israel's history serve as examples (or types) for us, Paul draws the parallel between God's provision for the Israelites in the wilderness and its fulfillment in Christ even closer: "They all ate the same spiritual food and drank the same spiritual drink; for they drank from the spiritual rock that accompanied them, and that rock was Christ" (1 Cor. 10:3–4).

Israel's deliverance from Egypt was not just a deliverance *out of* slavery, but they were also delivered *into* the Promised Land, the land where God caused his name to dwell. Thus they were brought to a place of fellowship with

19. Jean Daniélou, *From Shadows to Reality: Studies in the Biblical Typology of the Fathers*, trans. Dom Wulstan Hibberd (Westminster: Newman, 1960), 153.

God. Similarly, Christians are delivered from bondage to
sin, into fellowship with God through Jesus Christ (1 Cor.
1:8–9). Thus the place of rest and fellowship with God is no
longer a specific geographical area, but the person of Jesus
Christ prefigured by it.[20]

God had set Israel apart from the rest of the nations to
live in a special relationship with him (Lev. 20:24, 26). Indeed, Moses points out that God's presence with Israel distinguishes them from all the other people on the face of the
earth (Exod. 33:16). The commands, statutes, and ordi-
nances that regulated so much of Israelite life had much to
do with maintaining their distinctiveness and separateness
from the surrounding nations. This distinctiveness of Israel
points forward to the set-apartness of the community of believers in Christ. The apostle Paul, citing Old Testament
texts, makes this point to the church at Corinth:

> Do not be yoked together with unbelievers. For what
> do righteousness and wickedness have in common? Or
> what fellowship can light have with darkness? What har-
> mony is there between Christ and Belial? What does a
> believer have in common with an unbeliever? What
> agreement is there between the temple of God and
> idols? For we are the temple of the living God. As God
> has said: "I will live with them and walk among them,
> and I will be their God, and they will be my people."
>   "Therefore come out from them
>   and be separate,
>   says the Lord.

20. Leland Ryken, James C. Wilhoit, and Tremper Longman III, eds., *Dictionary
of Biblical Imagery* (Downers Grove, Ill.: InterVarsity, 1998), s.v. "Land" (488): "To
a large extent the Old Testament preoccupation with land as the locus of longing
and covenant blessing is replaced in the New Testament by Christ and his [*sic*] the
kingdom of God."

>   Touch no unclean thing,
>   and I will receive you."
>   "I will be a Father to you,
>   and you will be my sons and daughters,
>   says the Lord Almighty." (2 Cor. 6:14–18)

In spite of repeated calls by the prophets for her to repent, and warnings of dire consequences should she fail to do so, Israel subsequently turns away from God. As a result, she is listed together with the rest of the nations as being forced to drink from the cup of God's wrath (Jer. 25:15–26). Not only does this image of the cup of God's wrath find fulfillment in the cup Jesus agonizingly accepts from the Father (Luke 22:42), but it also points toward the coming judgment in which even the church will participate.[21] We are told in the New Testament that the church will be judged in the last day. Not only will the work of Christians be tested by fire (1 Cor. 3:12–15), but also the unbelievers will be weeded out of the church. New Testament passages use images of goats being separated out from the sheep (Matt. 25:31–46) and weeds being rooted out of the wheat (Matt. 13:24–30). There are many in the church who profess Christ, but do not really know him (Matt. 7:21–23). These will be removed in the final judgment, while the purified church remains.

Finally, the Old Testament account of Israel ends with a description of a remnant that survives the judgment and returns to the land/fellowship with God. While those who returned to the land after the exile were no more faithful to the covenant than were those who did not, their return was nec-

---

21. John T. Willis, "Some Suggestions on the Interpretation of Micah 1:2," *VT* 18/3 (1968): 378: "The prophets considered Yahweh's punishment of Israel a model or pattern for Yahweh's future punishment of the nations. The nations are to see Yahweh's *witness against* (accusation of) them (vv. 2–4) in His punishment of His own people (vv. 5–7)."

essary to indicate prophetically the faithful remnant of both Jews and Gentiles that would withstand the judgment of the church—the separation of the sheep and goats, the wheat and the tares—to be brought into everlasting fellowship with God.

The discontinuation of further scriptural revelation following the remnant's return and establishment upon the land signals the end of Israel's prophetic function of representing the nations, precisely because she has comprehensively communicated God's entire redemptive plan for humanity in Christ by her national experiences. With the end of the spoken and enacted prophecy, the unfolding of that redemptive plan begins, and we move to the New Testament manifestation of its realization in Jesus Christ. Israel's typological purpose, therefore, has been fulfilled, and the type must give way to the antitype:

The natural Israel, then, as God's chosen people from among the peoples of the earth, were types of the elect seed, the spiritual and royal priesthood, whom Christ was to choose out of the world, and redeem for His everlasting kingdom. When this latter purpose began to be carried into effect, the former, as a matter of course, began to give way—precisely as the shedding of Christ's blood upon the cross antiquated the whole sacrificial system of Moses. Hence, to indicate that the type, in this respect, has passed into the antitype, believers in Christ, of Gentile as well as of Jewish origin, are called Abraham's seed.[22]

22. Fairbairn, *The Typology of Scripture*, 1:416. See also Jean Daniélou, *Origen*, trans. Walter Mitchell (New York: Sheed and Ward, 1955), 150–51, who demonstrates that this was Origen's understanding of the relationship between the Old and New Testaments as well: "And so we come to the very heart of the mystery of the Christian interpretation of history, the meeting-point of symbolism and drama, of progress and the Cross. As Christians see it, history is symbolical. It is not a suc-

While we have not been able to highlight the typological significance of every detail of Israel's historical existence, what we have been able to survey has established beyond dispute that the accounts of Israel's experiences recorded for us in Scripture are extremely purposeful. They have been carefully selected and arranged (as, indeed, have the accounts of the individual prophets) to communicate a larger reality than that which Israel experienced. God chose the nation of Israel to be the transmitters and demonstrators of the broad outlines of his redemptive program in Jesus Christ.[23] Admittedly, it is impossible to believe that the Israelites realized to any great degree the role they were fulfilling or the significance of the message they were conveying. Nevertheless, they fulfilled the task, often in spite of themselves, and effectively laid before the nations, in the inspired text of their struggles, a visual drama in which they prophetically enacted through actual historical experiences a divine plan of salvation that gives comprehension to the entire Old Covenant.

We must not fail to note at this point that this view of Israel's typological significance is not new. In fact, it is very an-

---

cession of heterogeneous events. It constitutes a plan, every stage of which is at once an advance on its predecessor and a continuation of it. Only so does history cease to be dominated by brute fact and become an intelligible process and a possible object for contemplation from the religious point of view. . . . But there can be no progress in history without the destruction of what went before. In so far as the old order has an individual existence of its own it must be destroyed, if the new order is ever to come into being. Judaism had to be destroyed before the Church could come into being. . . . The old Temple had to be destroyed before the new Temple could make its appearance. . . . It thus becomes perfectly clear what the enmity the Jews felt toward Christ really meant: it was the visible embodiment of the refusal of the figure to accept its own dissolution."

23. T. H. L. Parker, *Calvin's Old Testament Commentaries* (Edinburgh: T. & T. Clark, 1986), 74–75, states that for Calvin "the history of the Jews was not only a preparation for the coming of Christ; it was also a deliberate pre-enactment of him and his work."

cient and well represented in the writings of the early Church Fathers. It is, for example, the view of Origen (ca. 185–255)[24] and others before him.[25] The typological significance of Israel's history in all its fullness can be traced back even further, as we have demonstrated, to the pages of the New Testament itself. We are not, therefore, *discovering* anything new, but rather *recovering* a spiritually rich perspective from which to view the entire Old Testament.

As fascinating, even enlightening, as all of this is, we must still ask what bearing it has on the present responsibilities of the church. In the words of my students, "So, how can I preach this?" While our answer to this question occupies much of the content of the final chapter, we may draw a general inference here. Because the nation of Israel bore a prophetic responsibility to point toward God's redemptive activity in the future involving both Christ and his church, it is reasonable and necessary to conclude that the covenant community that Israel typified also has a prophetic responsibility. Recognizing both what a prophet is and how he performs his various functions, as well as recognizing the fact that a community can effectively carry out prophetic functions, should orient, inform, and make effective the church's activity in the world today.

---

24. *De Principiis* 4.2.8: "But the most wonderful thing is, that by means of stories of wars and the conquerors and the conquered certain secret truths are revealed to those who are capable of examining these narratives; and, even more marvelous, through a written system of law the laws of truth are prophetically indicated, all these having been recorded in a series with a power which is truly appropriate to the wisdom of God." Commenting on the basis for Origen's interpretations of Scripture, Henri Crouzel (*Origen,* trans. A. S. Worrall [San Francisco: Harper and Row, 1989], 64) notes: "Varied as they are, there is regularly to be found a common basis for the spiritual exegeses: that the Old Testament in its entirety is a prophecy of Christ, who is the key to it."

25. Daniélou, *Origen,* 140: "His [i.e., Origen's] views on the [relationship between the two Testaments] simply represent the tradition . . . met with in Justin [ca. 100–166], Irenaeus [ca. 130–200] and Clement [ca. 150–215]."

Before we give some consideration to the details involved in such a prophetic engagement of the church with the world today, we need to make sure that we have not gotten ahead of ourselves or jumped the rails somewhere along the way. We therefore pause in our journey of discovery to focus our attention back on the touchstone for all of our Christian endeavors—Jesus Christ. How does this focal point of redemptive history and this mediator of the New Covenant inform our understanding of the prophetic office and the prophetic responsibilities of those who are united with him by faith? We explore the answers to this question in the next chapter.

FOR FURTHER REFLECTION

1. What parallels do you see between Israel's encounters with her ancient Near Eastern neighbors and the church's encounters with popular culture?
2. How has Israel fulfilled her prophetic calling in your life?
3. Is God's message limited by the willingness of the person or community he calls to prophesy? Explain.
4. How does an understanding of Israel's prophetic/ typological function affect your reading of the Old Testament?
5. Think of the parallels between Israel's prophetic function and that of the church. How might the church carry out her prophetic task today?

FIVE

THE CONSUMMATE PROPHET: JESUS CHRIST

There is, of course, always the danger that we may unconsciously impose our own framework of understanding on the biblical data in such a way that we end up making the evidence support what we already believe! Although this procedure may be satisfying as we find numerous apparent proofs of what we have concluded beforehand, it hardly establishes the legitimacy of our conclusions. What we need in order to guard ourselves against this dangerous course is some sort of exegetical check to make sure that we have not gone astray in our efforts to understand the biblical prophets. This exegetical check must be objective, and it must be provided by the Bible itself. Thankfully, such an exegetical check does exist, but it presupposes a certain understanding of the nature of Scripture that is not shared by everyone—not even every Christian. So, forthrightness demands that this implicit presupposition concerning the nature of Scripture be made explicit at the very start of our conversation.

This presupposition is simply that all of Scripture is divinely delivered redemptive revelation. Such a grammatically simple statement is loaded with fundamental theological implications. First, it implies that Scripture has an ultimately divine source. It is special *revelation* proceeding from God himself. As Louis Berkhof correctly notes: "God does not leave it to man to discover the knowledge of Him and of divine things, but actively and explicitly conveys this to man by means of his self-revelation."[1] This is the clear testimony of Scripture (2 Tim. 3:16; 2 Peter 1:20–21) and the historical witness of the church.[2] While it is fashionable in some circles these days to dispute the divine authority of Scripture, to do so merely renders all subsequent conversation irrelevant. Once we have rejected Scripture's own testimony about itself and millennia of the church's agreement with that testimony, we are thrust upon the shifting seas of our own subjective opinions where anyone's belief is unassailable, however outlandish it may be. Being unwilling to subject myself or you to such an unprofitable morass, and convicted of the truth of Scripture's claims,[3] I proceed with the traditional view.

Second, this statement implies that the divine purpose of this special revelation is *redemptive* in nature.[4] God has not

---

1. Louis Berkhof, *Introduction to Systematic Theology* (Grand Rapids: Baker, 1979 reprint), 96.

2. See, for example, the Belgic Confession, article 3; and the Westminster Confession of Faith, chapter 1.

3. This conviction comes by way of the Holy Spirit. See Calvin, *Institutes,* 1.7.4: "If we desire to provide in the best way for our consciences—that they may not be perpetually beset by the instability of doubt or vacillation, and that they may not also boggle at the smallest quibbles—we ought to seek our conviction [of the truth of Scripture] in a higher place than human reasons, judgments, or conjectures, that is, in the secret testimony of the Spirit."

4. Berkhof, *Introduction to Systematic Theology,* 138: "The proximate aim of revelation . . . is found in the complete renewal of sinners, in order that they may mirror the virtues and perfections of God."

revealed certain selected events from the past in an arbitrary fashion or to satisfy the idle historical interests of his curious human creations. Rather he has gone to this effort graciously to lead people back to a relationship with him and so repair the damage humankind introduced into his orderly, good world by means of our sin. All of our interpretive efforts must center on this redemptive nature of Scripture. Failure to grasp this important principle will cause us to miss the intended message while we're busy looking for things the Bible was never intended to provide.

Third, this special redemptive revelation of God finds its focus in the quintessential redemptive act of Jesus Christ, who, in his person, makes possible the redemption initiated by God and revealed in his Word.[5] Thus all of the Old Testament—the redemptive revelation of God—finds its focus in the culminating redemptive act of God in Jesus Christ. In the words of Berkhof:

> All the facts of the redemptive history that is recorded in the Bible center in that great fact [i.e., the redemptive act of God in Jesus Christ]. The various lines of the Old Testament revelation converge towards it, and those of the New Testament revelation radiate from it. It is only in their binding center, Jesus Christ, that the narratives of Scripture find

---

5. Report 44: "The Nature and Extent of Biblical Authority," *Agenda,* 1972 Synod of the Christian Reformed Church, 376–77: "There is a single plan of redemption and the whole of revelation points in that direction. Hence the history of redemption as recorded in the Bible can be characterized as the saving revelation of God in Jesus Christ. From its beginning to its end, from the beginning of history to the final coming of the kingdom, the history of redemption moves toward and flows from Jesus Christ. Thus the only correct understanding of the tremendous variety contained within Scripture is that which interprets it in its relationship to Jesus Christ. He is its unifying theme."

their explanation. The interpreter will truly understand them only insofar as he discerns their connection with the great central fact of Sacred History.[6]

JESUS PERFECTLY REPRESENTS GOD

Since our Lord is the focus of redemptive revelation, our
understanding of a prophet, which we have argued derives
from Scripture itself, must find not only some recognizable
expression in the life and work of Jesus Christ, but even its
ultimate expression. That is to say, Christ not only fulfills
Old Testament prophecy, but also perfectly fulfills the very
office of prophet. Every representative task characterizing
the prophetic office, therefore, we must find Jesus doing to
perfection, or else our understanding of a prophet has gone
off the rails somewhere back along the track. Let's carefully
consider, therefore, the ministry of Jesus and observe how it
follows the outline of the prophetic representational functions we have been considering.

Verbally
The first representative task of a prophet that we will
consider with respect to Jesus is that of representing God
with words. When we examine the passages of Scripture that
deal with Jesus' communication of the word of God, we already notice a departure from the Old Testament prophets'
performance of this task. The departure, as expected, is in
the direction of advancement or heightening. For example,
Jesus' authority to explain the essential concerns underlying
the specific points of the law is manifested in his incisive remarks in the Sermon on the Mount. In this penetrating
commentary on the law, Jesus goes beneath the explicit legal

6. Berkhof, *Principles of Biblical Interpretation,* 142.

proscriptions to address the deeper and broader concerns that underlie them. He repeatedly uses the authoritative phrase: "You have heard that it was said. . . . But *I* tell you . . . " (Matt. 5:21–22, 27–28, 33–34, 38–39, 43–44). The crowd correctly perceives that such statements resonate with an authority lacking in their own teachers. Upon hearing Jesus' powerful words, the crowd reacts with amazement, "because he taught as one who had authority, and not as their teachers of the law" (Matt. 7:28–29).

Even as a young boy, Jesus, sitting among the teachers in the temple courts, amazes his hearers with his understanding and his answers (Luke 2:41–47). This amazement at Jesus' ability to explain the Scriptures is experienced again later when the Sadducees test him with a question concerning the resurrection (Matt. 22:33). We may multiply such scriptural examples, but we need look no further than the clear statement of Jesus himself, who describes his proclamation as a perfect verbal representation of God, precisely communicating with words the message entrusted to him by the Father: "He who sent me is reliable, and what I have heard from him I tell the world. . . . I do nothing on my own but speak just what the Father has taught me" (John 8:26, 28).

Even though such statements indicate how perfectly Jesus fulfills this prophetic function, we can say even more. For the Scriptures testify that Jesus goes far beyond the prophetic task of *speaking* the words of God; he has become nothing less than the very embodiment of the Word of God. Thus Jesus is rightly called *the Word*. He not only speaks the word of God with a power and authority far beyond his predecessors; he, in fact, *is* that Word—the divine λόγος (*logos*)—who has become flesh and dwelt among us (John 1). His incarnation not only fulfills prophecy, but is also the perfect fulfillment of this representational task of the prophetic office.

Behaviorally

That such complete and perfect fulfillment of the prophetic office is not limited to the verbal dimension is apparent when Jesus' behaviors are considered. Our study of the biblical prophets revealed that a prophet represents God not only by words to the community of which he is a member, but also by his deeds. If this conclusion is correct, we should also be able to see in the recorded activity of Jesus, the consummate prophet, behaviors that demonstrate God's message to a perfect degree.

When the prophets seek to communicate a message from God behaviorally, they are usually limited to symbolic action. There are rare instances of the earlier, nonwriting prophets performing miracles, such as those performed by Elijah and Elisha, but by their very definition these miracles are exceptions to the prophets' regular functions, and are entirely absent from the recorded words and activities of the later, writing prophets. Therefore, except for the unusual and infrequent cases of miracles, when the prophets communicate their divine messages behaviorally, they perform symbolic acts. Indeed, it could not be otherwise. Even though these specially chosen and called human beings are given the extraordinary responsibility of representing God through their actions, they are nevertheless still human beings. These imperfect and limited human beings must therefore portray the actions of an almighty and unlimited God with symbols.

Of course, this is not the case with the Son of God, who is both fully human and fully divine. Because he is both God and man, Jesus' representative actions can far surpass the preceding prophets whose office he now perfectly executes. Jesus' actions perfectly represent God to his community because they are, after all, also divine acts. While providing a comprehensive catalog of actions he performs to demonstrate the truth of his messianic claim is unnecessary here, we may point to just a few to confirm this point.

In Matthew 9:1–8, some men bring a paralytic to Jesus to be healed. Responding favorably to this demonstration of their faith, Jesus announces to the paralytic that his sins are forgiven. Within the onlooking crowd, some teachers of the law express their shock that Jesus would make such a declaration reserved for God alone, and so accuse him of blasphemy. Jesus responds to this false charge in a way that demonstrates the synergy of his words and actions. In order to communicate visually as well as verbally the reality of the good news that was being expressed among them, Jesus subsequently adds to the paralytic's spiritual healing a physical one as well. As Jesus puts it to the unbelieving spectators, "So that you may know that the Son of Man has authority on earth to forgive sins. . . ." Thus his actions are intended to communicate the reality to which his words also point; namely, that God has come in the person of his Son to redeem his people.

Jesus explicitly states that his behaviors, his divine acts, his miracles, are intended to serve as another channel through which he communicates the truth of his divine redemptive mission. In Jerusalem, during the Feast of Dedication, Jesus is pressed by a crowd to tell them clearly if he is the Christ. To this demand Jesus, surely exasperated by this time, gives an answer that reveals the communicative intent of his actions: "I did tell you, but you do not believe. *The miracles I do in my Father's name speak for me*" (John 10:25).

Thus, unlike the prophets who had preceded him, whose actions were also performed in order to communicate the divine will, Jesus is not limited to symbolic measures that are restricted by their very symbolism. Rather, Jesus' miracles are direct manifestations of divine power that serve as proof of his claims to be the Son of God, while also serving to provide visible demonstrations of the reality of the deliverance from sin and its effects that he has come to inaugurate.

In the course of his oration to the assembled crowd on the day of Pentecost (Acts 2:14–41), the apostle Peter explains that the miracles performed by Jesus were precisely for this purpose: "Men of Israel, listen to this: Jesus of Nazareth was a man accredited by God to you by miracles, wonders and signs, which God did among you through him, as you yourselves know" (Acts 2:22). The word translated as "accredited" in this verse is ἀποδεδειγμένον (*apode-deigmenon*), which is the perfect passive participle of ἀποδείκνυμι (*apodeiknymi*), meaning "to proclaim, demonstrate, or prove."[7] In other words, the miracles, wonders, and signs performed by Jesus are God's proclamation, demonstration, or proof of Jesus' verbal claims to divinity.

The most significant miracle of all, to which the New Testament authors repeatedly point, is Jesus' resurrection from the dead. Paul the apostle affirms that this grand event, too, most mightily and effectively testifies to Jesus' divinity. In Romans 1:4 Paul states that Jesus "was declared with power to be the Son of God by his resurrection from the dead." That is to say, the *act* of the resurrection *declares* the unmistakable message that Jesus is God.

We must therefore be careful not to regard Jesus' miracles as simply fascinating, but ultimately peripheral and capricious exhibitions of divine power. The miracles Jesus performs are intentional, calculated, and integrally connected with the verbal message he proclaims. Both his words *and* his actions are communication, which represents God to his human creations in the clearest possible terms. In his

---

7. J. H. Moulton and G. Milligan, *Vocabulary of the Greek Testament* (Peabody, Mass.: Hendrickson, 1930), and G. Abbott-Smith, *A Manual Greek Lexicon of the New Testament* (Edinburgh: T. & T. Clark, 1981).

words and his actions, therefore, Jesus is fulfilling the office of prophet by representing God. There is yet, however, another aspect of God's being that Jesus represents to us.

Affectively

Like the Old Testament prophets before him, Jesus also represents in his physical being the affections of God. Although this feature of Jesus' ministry is often overlooked, God, in his grand condescension to communicate to his beloved creatures the full-bodied message of redemption in its most comprehensive expression, does not limit himself only to the cognitive dimension. He reaches out to humankind on every level of our existence. So, through his prophets, and especially through the One who perfectly fulfills the prophetic office, God conveys to his creatures his own emotions, ranging from love and compassion to anger.

Jesus' (and, therefore, God's) compassion for his people is demonstrated repeatedly throughout his ministry[8] and is perhaps most clearly expressed by his weeping over Jerusalem (Luke 19:41). In this passage, Jesus, expressing God's own concern, weeps over the coming consequences of his people's unbelief.[9] This coming destruction of Jerusalem, which would occur as a necessary judgment of sin,[10] harkens back to the previous destruction of Jerusalem at the hands of the Babylonian troops under the command of Nebuchadnezzar in 586 B.C. This previous destruction too was foretold by the prophet Isaiah in words that communicate the overwhelming emotion of God at the necessity of bringing such a calamity against his own people: "Turn

8. See, for example, Matt. 9:36; 14:14 (parallel in Mark 6:34); 15:32 (parallel in Mark 8:2); 20:34.

9. Jesus had expressed a similar concern earlier in Luke 13:34–35.

10. This would occur in A.D. 70, when Roman troops invaded and leveled the rebellious Jewish province of Judea.

away from me; let me weep bitterly. Do not try to console me over the destruction of my people" (Isa. 22:4).

We see the anger or wrath of God displayed in Jesus' violent response toward the actions of those who would lead others into lowering their reverence and esteem for the dwelling place of God to casual marketplace attitudes. The apostle John records for us this divine anger in his Gospel:

> When it was almost time for the Jewish Passover, Jesus went up to Jerusalem. In the temple courts he found men selling cattle, sheep and doves, and others sitting at tables exchanging money. So he made a whip out of cords, and drove all from the temple area, both sheep and cattle; he scattered the coins of the money changers and overturned their tables. To those who sold doves he said, "Get these out of here! How dare you turn my Father's house into a market!" His disciples remembered that it is written: "Zeal for your house will consume me." (John 2:13–17)

Jesus reacts similarly to the Pharisees and those teachers of the law whose scrupulous adherence to the letter of divine and human law had blinded them to the underlying principles that those laws embodied. In their own personal behavior, therefore, as well as in what they taught others by word and example, they had substituted activity for attitude, manner for mercy, and habit for heart. In a clear demonstration of God's outrage over this perversion of the true intent of his instructions, Jesus describes these people as hypocrites, sons of hell, blind guides, blind fools, whitewashed tombs, snakes, and a brood of vipers (Matt. 23:1–36)—harsh language indeed! These emotionally charged words on the part of his perfect representative reveal the gravity of this matter to God, and to us, and give us another glimpse of divine emotion.

Completely

As in the case of the prophets of the Old Testament, the words, actions, and affections of Jesus cannot be separated from one another in actual experience as we have artificially done here. All of these aspects of God's perfect representative operate together in a complex dynamic in order to communicate his message. The verbal (words), behavioral (actions), and affective (emotions) dimensions are all fully utilized to convey the divine will and express the divine personality in ways that cannot fail to be comprehended. When Philip, the disciple of Jesus, asks him to "show us the Father," Jesus points out, somewhat disappointedly we assume, that he has been doing exactly that by means of the totality of his ministry. He encourages Philip to accept the message not only of his words, but also of his actions:

> How can you say, "Show us the Father"? Don't you believe that I am in the Father, and that the Father is in me? The words I say to you are not just my own. Rather, it is the Father, living in me, who is doing his work. Believe me when I say that I am in the Father and the Father is in me; *or at least believe on the evidence of the miracles themselves.* (John 14:9–11)

It is clear from his response to Philip's question that Jesus intends his entire life, in all of its aspects, to be a manifestation of the Father and to give unambiguous expression to his message of salvation.

Jesus gives much the same response to a doubtful John the Baptist (Matt. 11:2–6; Luke 7:18–23), who, while in prison, sends his disciples to ask of Jesus, "Are you the one who was to come, or should we expect someone else?" This question manifests no small degree of uncertainty regarding the divine message Jesus is at pains to communicate with the entirety of his being. Jesus responds to John's query by encouraging him to receive and accept the truth of this multi-dimensional communication that he is conveying by both words (things heard) and actions (things seen). Thus he tells John's disciples, "Go back and report to John *what you hear and see*." The things seen are the miracles Jesus performs, representing the divine presence in power, and the thing heard is "the good news preached to the poor." That is to say, there is nothing about Jesus' life that does not contribute to the divine message he brings.

We have been considering the direction of prophetic representation that proceeds from God to his people, and we have shown that every area that we have observed to be operative for Old Testament prophets also applies to the One who fulfills the prophetic office. However, Jesus carries all of the representative aspects of a prophet further to the point of executing them in the fullest and most perfect fashion possible. This is stated succinctly by the author of the book of Hebrews, who puts it this way:

> In the past God spoke to our forefathers through the prophets at many times and in various ways, but in these last days he has spoken to us by his Son, whom he appointed heir of all things, and through whom he made the universe. The Son is the radiance of God's glory and *the exact representation of his being*, sustaining all things by his powerful word. (Heb. 1:1–3)

Jesus, who fulfills the prophetic office, confirms our understanding of the prophetic task of representing God

through words, actions, and affections by doing these things
to perfection himself. Yet we have also to consider the other
direction of the prophet's task: representing the community
of which he was a member, also by words, actions, and affections.

JESUS PERFECTLY REPRESENTS
HIS COMMUNITY

The title of this subsection presumes something fantastic. So before we plunge into a consideration of the specifics
of whether and how Jesus fulfills this prophetic task, we need
to examine this presumption a little more closely, for so
much depends on it. It requires no great mental ability on
our part to identify the Old Testament prophets as members
of the community of Israel. They belong to the same ethnic
group, participate in the same national experiences, and, of
course, share in a common humanity. The same, however,
could not have been said of God before the incarnation.
That is not to say that God did not have a relationship with
his chosen people. He had gone to great lengths to establish
his covenant with Israel. Yet God did not share their ethnic-
ity, or even their humanity, for the simple reason that God is
not human. A prophet represents the community of which
he is a member. How then could God, not being human,
fully identify with the segment of human population on
whose behalf he would fulfill the prophetic task of representation? This is a huge problem with implications far beyond
academic curiosity.

For God to carry out perfectly the prophetic task of representation, he would have to become human in order to
share in the humanity and the experiences of the people he
would represent. That Jesus must represent the community
he came to save is referred to by theologians as the necessity

of the incarnation. For Jesus to be the Messiah and earn our salvation, he would have to represent his people in obedience (Rom. 5:18–19), represent us in experiencing the penalty of sin (Heb. 2:14–17), represent us to God (1 Tim. 2:5), and represent us in resurrection (1 Cor. 15:23).[11] For this representation to be real and effective, God would have to enter into physical human existence. Thus God, in his unfathomable compassion and mercy, and in a mysterious and holy way, did indeed become flesh and dwell among us in the person of Jesus Christ (John 1:14; Phil. 2:6–8). He became like us in every respect, save for sin (Heb. 4:15). So, not only could Jesus rightly be called the Son of God, but also the Son of Man. The significance of these dual titles becomes evident when we reflect upon the representational functions of the prophets.

Verbally

As one who shares in our humanity, Jesus represents us with words. Perhaps the most well known instance of this is Jesus' "high-priestly prayer" recorded in the seventeenth chapter of John's Gospel. In verses 6–19 Jesus represents his disciples verbally by means of intercessory prayer. He goes on to say, in verse 20, that his prayer is not only for his current disciples, but "also for those who will believe in me through their message"; that is, for all present and future disciples of Christ. Furthermore, we should not think that Jesus' intercession on behalf of believers ceases with his crucifixion. On the contrary, Jesus rose from the dead and ascended to the right hand of the Father, with whom he continues to intercede for us (Rom. 8:34). In a later letter, John assures those believers who sin that "we have one who

11. Wayne Grudem, *Systematic Theology: An Introduction to Biblical Doctrine* (Grand Rapids: Zondervan, 1994), 540–43.

speaks to the Father in our defense—Jesus Christ, the Righteous One" (1 John 2:1). Moreover, whereas human prophets interceded with God on behalf of his people, Jesus, the perfect prophet, takes this even further. His intercession is unimpeded by sin and continuous. The author of Hebrews tells us that Jesus "is able to save completely those who come to God through him, because he *always lives to intercede for them*" (7:25). Jesus' prophetic intercession for his people is as eternal and perfect as he is.

But as is the case for the prophets of the Old Testament, Jesus' representation of his people extends far beyond intercessory prayer. Jesus embodies his community, his church, in the fullness of his very being. The Old Testament prophets also represented Israel with every facet of their lives, but Jesus' representation differs from that of the previous prophets in that he represents us to the perfect degree.

Behaviorally

Jesus' representative function in the behavioral area again surpasses that of the biblical prophets. The biblical prophets represent in their individual persons, by means of experiences and behaviors, what the nation as a whole could look forward to. That is, the prophets' own personal experiences represent future national experiences.

As mind-bending and revelatory as this representative function is, however, it is still limited by the fallen humanity of the prophet. When a biblical prophet represents God's judgment upon the nation's sin by means of certain behaviors, for example, his representation is necessarily symbolic. The prophet is unable *actually* to experience the judgment of the entire covenant community as their representative inasmuch as he is a finite and sinful human being who can do no more than bear the punishment for his own sin. Thus, his representation of divine judgment is necessarily *symbolic*.

What is needed for there to be a true representative of God's people, who can bear an infinite divine wrath against all human sin in their place, is a human being who is also God—a sinless human being capable of *actually* experiencing God's just punishment for the collective sin of humankind as a true representative of his people. This actual (instead of simply symbolic) representative, Jesus Christ, infinitely surpasses the prophets' abilities within this representative sphere. Christ's actual representation of his community in his experience of the divine judgment against sin is summarized by the author of Hebrews with these words:

> Since the children have flesh and blood, he [i.e., Christ] too shared in their humanity so that by his death he might destroy him who holds the power of death—that is, the devil—and free those who all their lives were held in slavery by their fear of death. For surely it is not angels he helps, but Abraham's descendants. For this reason he had to be made like his brothers in every way, in order that he might become a merciful and faithful high priest in service to God, and that he might make atonement for the sins of the people. (Heb. 2:14–17)

This suffering of Christ as our representative is credited to us as though we actually experienced it. His suffering also represents what the church can expect to experience, albeit to a much lesser degree no matter how horrendous it is in human terms. Jesus clarifies this additional representative dimension of his suffering in his words to his disciples:

> If the world hates you, keep in mind that it hated me first. If you belonged to the world, it would love you

as its own. As it is, you do not belong to the world, but I have chosen you out of the world. That is why the world hates you. Remember the words I spoke to you: "No servant is greater than his master." If they persecuted me, they will persecute you also. (John 15:18–20)[12]

The perfect prophet, our perfect representative, represents his people not only in his experience of the divine wrath on their behalf, but also by his resurrection from the dead. The Scriptures make it clear that Christ's resurrection is at the same time a revelation of divine power and a revelation of what the community of God's people may also expect for themselves already in the present and experience in its fullness at his return. The believer's present participation in the reality that Christ's own resurrection portends consists in the new life that our union with him generates. In his letter to the church at Rome the apostle Paul describes the new life of the believer in terms of the resurrection:

We were . . . buried with him through baptism into death in order that, just as Christ was raised from the dead through the glory of the Father, we too may live a new life. If we have been united with him like this in his death, we will certainly also be united with him in his resurrection. For we know that our old self was crucified with him so that the body of sin might be done away with, that we should no longer be slaves to sin—because anyone who has died has been freed from sin. (Rom. 6:4–7)[13]

12. See also Rom. 8:17; 2 Cor. 1:5; Phil. 1:29; 3:10; 2 Tim. 3:12; 1 Peter 4:12–16.
13. See also Eph. 2:4–6; Col. 3:1–4.

While believers already experience the resurrection in part by means of their new life in Christ, because Jesus physically rose from the dead, we may also look forward to our own physical resurrection. Jesus indicates in his own person what *all* believers will experience, and so performs the prophetic function of representing the community by his action—in this case, by his resurrection. The fact of his resurrection ensures the fact of every believer's resurrection. The Bible uses the term "firstfruits" to describe this representative character of Jesus' resurrection:

> Christ has indeed been raised from the dead, the firstfruits of those who have fallen asleep. For since death came through a man, the resurrection of the dead comes also through a man. For as in Adam all die, so in Christ all will be made alive. But each in his own turn: Christ, the firstfruits; then, when he comes, those who belong to him. (1 Cor. 15:20–23)

Thus, in addition to his other prophetic functions, Christ fulfills the representative role of the prophet by representing the community with his actions, especially manifest in the resurrection. That is the glorious and certain expectation of every Christian precisely because of its representative quality.

Affectively

We may even observe physical and psychological states or conditions in Jesus that correspond to those of the community he represents. While an exhaustive list of these is unnecessary here, we may point to passages that speak of physical states such as hunger (Matt. 4:2; 21:18) and fatigue (Matt. 8:20). Such elements of his humanity further substantiate that in addition to being the Son of God, Jesus is also the Son of Man. He has fully identified himself with the human condition and is therefore able to represent fully the human community he came to redeem.

In addition to representative physical states, Jesus also demonstrates those psychical traits that should come to characterize the covenant community. We observe, for example, Jesus' compassion for the spiritual and physical condition of others (Matt. 9:36; 14:14; 15:32; 20:34), and recognize the compassion that should distinguish the life of believers, who love their neighbors as themselves (Matt. 19:19), and which informs the church's emphasis on social as well as spiritual concerns.

We see Jesus' anger at sin when he turns over the tables of the moneychangers in the temple (Matt. 21:12–13; Mark 11:15–17; Luke 19:45–46) and when insincere listeners try to trap him with words (Matt. 22:18). This refusal to accept a spirituality reduced to a mere form of godliness that denies or ignores the substance of faith finds echoes elsewhere in the New Testament (2 Tim. 4:3–4) and calls believers to a continual self-examination and sustained dissatisfaction with sin in our own lives.

Jesus also, of course, experienced the anguish and sorrow associated with his terrible suffering on our behalf, and even with its anticipation. In Gethsemane, Jesus told his disciples that his "soul is overwhelmed with sorrow to the point of death" (Matt. 26:38). Then came the anticipated dreadful suffering with spitting, slapping, mocking, a crown of thorns, beating, and finally crucifixion (Matt. 26:67–68; 27:27–50). Before this frightful end, however, Jesus had made it clear that even in his suffering he was indicating what lay in store for the community he represented. That is, his suffering, as we have already observed, has a representative dimension.

The church may also learn from the joy that Jesus experienced, for this too is representational. In John 15:11 and 17:13 Jesus refers to his joy. The author of Hebrews notes that this joy was "set before" Jesus, and was the motivation for him to endure the cross (12:2). In his discussion of this verse, John Owen suggests that the joy set before Jesus was the prospect of future glory.[14] Thus his desire for the church to know his joy is a desire that we too might experience already in our present circumstances, however unpleasant they may be, the joy that God has prepared for us.[15] Jesus' joy, therefore, represents the joy that is to characterize the community that bears his name.[16]

CONCLUSION

We have seen a consistent pattern throughout the Old Testament that finds its fulfillment in Jesus Christ. From the individual prophets to the nation of Israel to the One who fulfills this redemptive revelation perfectly, the prophetic functions of representation have been carried out in exactly the same way. We have seen not only that it is possible for a community to carry out the prophetic functions, but that this already has been done (and is continuing to be done) by Israel through its divinely directed, recorded, and preserved experiences that have been providentially delivered to us today in the pages of the sacred text. It is time, therefore, for

14. John Owen makes these remarks in connection with his translation of John Calvin, *Commentaries on the Epistle of Paul the Apostle to the Hebrews* (1853; Grand Rapids: Baker, 1996 reprint), 395–96: "The subject handled is, that the prospect of future glory ought to sustain us under the evils of the present life; and Christ is referred to as an example."

15. Note that the immediate contexts of John 15:11, 17:13, and Heb. 12:2 involve obedience and hardship—hardly the contemporary church's understanding of the context of joy.

16. For a further discussion of Jesus' emotions, see Grudem, *Systematic Theology*, 533–34.

us as the contemporary people of God to take our place among this great cloud of witnesses and accept the mantle of prophetic responsibility that is appointed for us. It is thrilling to consider that we are participating in the communication of God's truth in ways practiced by the prophets of the Old Testament and modeled to perfection for us by our Lord. We, as the contemporary church, are an integral part of a historic witness designed by God and effectively carried out by his people throughout all ages. We have also been given a prophetic call by God to carry his truth into the world. It is vitally important not only that we willingly accept this charge, but do so with an understanding of all of its different dimensions so that we may be that much more effectively engaged in carrying it out.

How should the church practically engage in its prophetic calling in today's world? Now that we have some clearer idea of what that calling is all about, how can the church perform its prophetic task most faithfully to God and helpfully to those to whom it ministers? These are the fundamental questions that should be at the heart of every local church and inform and enthuse its programs, activities, worship, fellowship, and witness. In the next chapter, we begin to translate our biblically informed understanding of the church's prophetic role into practical avenues for its execution.

FOR FURTHER REFLECTION

1. How does the redemptive work of Jesus Christ serve as an exegetical check on our interpretation of Scripture?

2. Are those who claim that the Bible is a history book correct? How would you correct or modify their claim? On what basis would you do so?

SIX

THE PROPHETIC ROLE OF THE CHURCH

Before we jump headlong into a discussion of how to apply the things we've learned about the prophetic functions to the contemporary church, we should make sure that our conceptual bungee cords are attached securely. In other words, we need a common understanding of what we mean by the term "church" before we can meaningfully discuss anything about it. This step is vitally important because our perception of the local church—what we believe should take place within the worship service itself and what the role of each member within a specific congregation should be—has direct bearing on what we believe our role should be in the larger, universal church. If, for example, my understanding of adequate participation in the local church is regular attendance at roughly one-hour services (with occasional coffee and doughnuts afterward) and perhaps enough financial giving to avoid uncomfortable questions, then my understanding of my role in the larger, universal church would likely involve minimal time, effort, and money—hardly the whole-life commitment we have seen with the prophets. A reorientation of our perception of the local church, and our involvement in it, based on our understanding of prophetic functions will lead to a new appreciation and enthusiasm for our role in the universal church as well.

Current popular perceptions of what the church should be and do, however, number almost as many as the people who have them, and these perceptions are frequently, and unfortunately, built on other than biblical foundations. Peter Savage has noted four major models or misconceptions of the church that prevail to some degree in local congregations.[1] While these misconceptions of the church may strike some of us as unfamiliar and humorous, the sad fact is that many of our contemporary churches function as though these practical blunders were, in fact, legitimate expressions of the covenant community.

The first of these models or misconceptions holds that the church is primarily a *lecture hall*.[2] In this view of the church, people attend primarily to hear the Scripture expounded by a speaker. They sit quietly, hopefully attentive to the message/lecture delivered from the pulpit. The effectiveness of the church is decided on the basis of the degree to which the speaker can hold the audience's attention and interest. The worship service is largely unidirectional; that is, from God (by means of the preacher) to the congregation/audience. The idea of worship as a "dialogue" between God and his people[3] is not purposely incorporated into the liturgy to any signifi-

1. Peter Savage, "The Church and Evangelicalism," in *The New Face of Evangelicalism,* ed. C. René Padilla (Downers Grove, Ill.: InterVarsity, 1976), 106–20.

2. Rick Warren, *The Purpose-Driven Church: Growth Without Compromising Your Message and Mission* (Grand Rapids: Zondervan, 1995), 123–24, refers to this particular model as "the classroom church" and describes it as one in which "a pastor sees his primary role as being a teacher."

3. See, for example, the *Acts of Synod* (1968) for the Christian Reformed Church, Supplement 3, 134–98; especially p. 137: "Worship for the people of the living God has always been a dialogue."

cant degree. This concentration upon only one side of the divine-human conversation results in little involvement by the congregation within the church service itself, which translates, ultimately, into the perception on the part of the congregation that little involvement is required outside of the "classroom" as well. This model suggests that individual participation in the life and purpose of the church boils down to little more than regular attendance at weekly "services." While this model is perhaps rich in biblical content, there is little or no emphasis on what to do with that content in one's everyday life; there are few opportunities to apply it to practical situations. In other words, the surrounding culture is not meaningfully engaged—much less transformed—and that local church consequently fails to fulfill its prophetic calling to any significant degree.

The second model with which some operate is the church as a *variety show*. This perspective views the primary purpose of the weekly gathering of parishioners as their entertainment (though this is rarely, if ever, overtly stated). The church "service" is constructed to cater to this desire and boost attendance by being structured as a series of discrete, not necessarily related events or presentations, which are intended to hold the "audience's" attention and satisfy their "felt" needs for experiences of emotional uplifting and personal confirmation. This understanding of the church seeks to answer the question that is unfortunately primary in the minds of many attendees: "What did I get out of it?" This model brings with it the danger of superficial allegiance on the part of the church members, who will quickly abandon the church when it no longer provides the entertainment that satisfies them. It orients the parishioners to the idea that the church exists to make their lives as satisfying and enjoyable as possible. A church "service," in other words, is viewed above anything else as a "service" to the congregation. Obviously, this model does not promote a committed Christian lifestyle characterized by sacrifice and obedience.

A third model views the church as a *corporation*. This model is "efficient and highly program-oriented with a full-time pastoral team involved in retailing religion to the masses."[4] There is little flexibility in the operation of this religious corporation, and the gospel is viewed more as a product that needs to be sold than as a call for entrance into a new world characterized by fundamentally different patterns for being and acting. Outwardly there is little difference between how this model of the church functions and how any corporation functions. The pastor's "study" has been replaced by the pastor's "office," effectively communicating to the members the shift in emphasis from personal transformation to external institutional organization. This model also has the danger of suggesting to parishioners that there really is no fundamental difference between how the church should attract "customers" and how corporate America attracts customers. However, as we have seen, the prophetic task has little to do with business models.

The fourth model of the church that we should avoid holds up as primary the idea of fellowship. This is the model of the church as a *social club*.[5] While fellowship is certainly a biblical concept and should be present in any healthy congregation, how one understands fellowship is all-important.

---

4. Howard A. Snyder, *The Community of the King* (Downers Grove, Ill.: Inter-Varsity, 1977), 36. E. Glenn Wagner, *Escape from Church, Inc.: The Return of the Pastor-Shepherd* (Grand Rapids: Zondervan, 1999), 21, believes that "the one problem underlying all others [regarding the church] is that we have moved both pastors and churches from a community model to a corporation model. In some churches the pastor is the preaching machine while someone else runs the business side of things. In other churches the pastor is the CEO, the boss, the chairman of the board. But in both cases, the pastor is a corporate officer, not a shepherd."

5. Warren, *The Purpose-Driven Church,* 123, refers to this model as "the family reunion church" and describes it as "a church that focuses primarily on fellowship."

The biblical concept of fellowship involves mutual encouragement to continue in the faith and in faithful service to God, as well as communal support for the various trials each member will face in life. In the social club model of the church, however, fellowship has little to do with faith or mutual support. It is essentially understood as the gathering and socializing of people with similar likes, dislikes, and circumstances for group activities and fun. This model yields such peculiarities as the ladies' outing to the discount malls, the youth group trip to the ball game, and the men's fishing expedition. While any of these activities can certainly include mutual support and encouragement in comfortable group settings, such support and encouragement are not emphasized in this model. This understanding of the church downplays the revolutionary, life-changing character of the gospel and has the danger of turning gatherings of believers into merely social engagements. It also has the potential of being exclusivist. If someone does not "fit" into the social group currently gathering, that person is not welcomed but is made to understand, perhaps only in such subtle ways as a look or muttered remark, that somewhere else would be better for him or her. This results in such unbiblical consequences as white churches, black churches, Dutch churches, and rich churches, and runs counter to the barrier-free, universal gospel that heralds the formation of one new humanity out of a divided and broken world.

So how *should* we understand the church? Howard Snyder has suggested several important elements that we may consider together in formulating a useful and accurate definition of the church. These may be boiled down to the simple assertion that the church is *the charismatic community of the people of God*. The church is "charismatic" in the sense "that it exists by the grace (*charis*) of God and is built up by the gifts of grace (*charismata*) bestowed by the Spirit."[6] God calls the church into existence by his electing grace (Eph. 1:3–14). He ensures its proper growth by conferring upon its members spiritual gifts for the common good (1 Cor. 12:7).

The church is also a community, a fellowship, a *koinōnia*. However, this is not limited to the kind of fellowship or community that one would experience at a Super Bowl party. Rather, this fellowship of believers is nothing less than "the new humanity that Christ is creating," which "becomes visible in communities that have a quality of life that reflects Christ's example."[7] There should be a caring and encouraging atmosphere of mutual accountability in each congregation as we help each other on toward Christ-likeness. We need to display in our relationships the kind of humanity God intended.

Finally, the church comprises the people of God. The people of God are those whom God has called, has been transforming, and has been using in his grand redemptive work throughout history.[8] It is for the purpose of under-

6. Snyder, *The Community of the King*, 57.

7. Ibid., citing Samuel Escobar, "Evangelism and Man's Search for Freedom, Justice, and Fulfillment," in J. D. Douglas, ed., *Let the Earth Hear His Voice* (Minneapolis: World Wide Publications, 1975), 312. Note that already we are beginning to see connections between the role of the church and the representational functions of a prophet.

8. Snyder, *The Community of the King*, 56. Orlando E. Costas, *The Church and Its Mission: A Shattering Critique from the Third World* (Wheaton, Ill.: Tyndale, 1974), 44–45: "God has chosen the church to be preeminently a prophetic community. . . . As a prophetic community the church exists to proclaim 'the wonderful deeds of him who called [her] out of darkness into his marvelous light' (1 Pe. 2:9b). . . . In other words, the church's sovereign and merciful election to be the people of God is validated and fulfilled when she proclaims the mighty deeds of God. At the same time, the church can make this proclamation only *as* the people who have been set apart by God and for God. In this respect the church's proclamation is both an act of praise and thanksgiving as well as a testimony of her experience and merciful origin."

standing exactly how we should be actively participating in that redemptive work that we continue to explore the relationship between the prophetic representational task and the contemporary role of the church. Let us therefore explore how we may apply what we have seen to be the specific tasks of a prophet (demonstrated also by the community of Israel, and fulfilled in Christ) to this charismatic community of the people of God. After all, the apostle Paul tells us that "those God foreknew he also predestined to be conformed to the likeness of his Son" (Rom 8:29). If his Son perfectly fulfilled the prophetic office in the ways we have observed, it is logically inescapable that we too have a prophetic responsibility. If we are serious about participating in the process of conforming to Christ, we need to consider what becoming prophetic means for the contemporary church in practical terms.

THE CHURCH MUST REPRESENT GOD

The prophetic call, the specifics of which we examined in chapter 2, has clearly been given to the church. Remember that two key identifying elements of a prophetic call are the formal commission (usually signaled by the word "go" or "send") and divine reassurance (usually identified by the words "I will be with you"). It is no coincidence that we find exactly these two elements in the words of the Great Commission that Jesus gives to his disciples in Matthew 28:18–20: "All authority in heaven and on earth has been given to me. Therefore *go* and make disciples of all nations, baptizing them in the name of the Father and of the Son and of the Holy Spirit, and teaching them to obey everything I have commanded you. And surely *I am with you always,* to the very end of the age."

Other elements of the prophetic call are present as well.

Surely Jesus' incarnation qualifies as a *divine confrontation* without parallel. In the person of Jesus Christ, God meets with us. Even the very name "Immanuel," applied to Jesus in Matthew 1:23, is a transliteration of the Hebrew phrase אֵל + עִמָּנוּ (*'immanu* + *'el*), meaning very literally, "God with us." Jesus' verbal, behavioral, and affective communication during his earthly ministry constitutes the *introductory word,* by which he establishes his identity as God in the flesh and inaugurates the kingdom. We can even recognize something very like the prophet's *objection* to his calling in the reluctant, stuttering efforts of the church in carrying out the prophetic task in both ancient and modern times. Finally, the visible *sign* from God confirming his intent to use the prophet in his special service finds its parallel in the coming of the Holy Spirit on the day of Pentecost with "a sound like the blowing of a violent wind" and with "tongues of fire that separated and came to rest" on each of the apostles, who subsequently "began to speak in other tongues" (Acts 2:1–4). While he was speaking with his apostles before his ascension, Jesus clearly linked the visible coming of the Spirit with the church's witness in the world: "You will receive power when the Holy Spirit comes on you; and you will be my witnesses in Jerusalem, and in all Judea and Samaria, and to the ends of the earth" (Acts 1:8).

All of these indicators of a prophetic call make it impossible to miss the fact that the church, like the Old Testament prophets, has received the call to carry out the prophetic task, a task we see perfectly fulfilled by our Lord. Since Jesus perfectly fulfilled the functions of a prophet, and we are being conformed to his likeness, we also should be performing those same prophetic functions. So how should the church specifically carry out these prophetic tasks? Let's consider each of these representational responsibilities separately.

Verbally

One would have a difficult time denying that verbal representation is a fundamental aspect of the church's responsibility. Such verbal representation (or, more familiarly, "spreading the gospel") is the traditional understanding of the role of the church and comprises the bulk of what Christian education and ministry preparation are all about. In his description of the witness of New Testament Christians, Gene Getz lays particular emphasis on the diverse verbal component of their message: "They taught, declared, spoke, proclaimed, preached, testified, witnessed, exhorted, praised, reasoned, refuted, explained, demonstrated, persuaded, and gave evidence for what they believed."[9] Indeed, there are a variety of scripturally mandated ways to communicate the truth about God with words. Paul charges Timothy: *"Preach the word; be prepared in season and out of season; correct, rebuke and encourage*—with great patience and careful *instruction"* (2 Tim. 4:2). As Paul explains in his letter to the church at Rome, God uses words—namely, preaching—to call sinners to himself (Rom. 10:14–15): "How, then, can they call on the one they have not believed in? And how can they believe in the one of whom they have not heard? And how can they hear without someone preaching to them? And how can they preach unless they are sent? As it is written, 'How beautiful are the feet of those who bring good news!'"

Preaching has long been the centerpiece of the church's verbal representation and receives the greatest emphasis in our seminaries and churches. But, of course, the church's responsibility to represent God with words is not limited to preaching. We also must communicate the truth about God verbally in various other ways, including teaching. As Paul

---

9. Gene A. Getz, *Sharpening the Focus of the Church* (Chicago: Moody, 1974), 164.

instructs Timothy: "The Lord's servant must not quarrel; instead, he must be kind to everyone, able to *teach*, not resentful. Those who oppose him he must gently *instruct*, in the hope that God will grant them repentance leading them to a knowledge of the truth" (2 Tim. 2:24–25). Teaching is also an integral part of the Great Commission that the Lord gives to his disciples in Matthew 28:16–20: "Therefore go and make disciples of all nations, baptizing . . . and *teaching*. . . ." Imagine the renewed enthusiasm of Sunday school instructors, adult education speakers, Vacation Bible School leaders, Christian school teachers, and other educators within the church when they realize that what they are doing is an essential component of the prophetic task! Instead of a routine, unfulfilling exercise, their teaching becomes an avenue for the same prophetic verbal representation carried out by the prophets of the Old Testament, the nation of Israel, and our Lord. They can begin to see themselves in the stream of redemptive witness flowing from God's people of the past and forward to the consummation. They are fulfilling the church's prophetic calling to represent God with words.

Another way to fulfill this calling, also commanded in the Great Commission, is by means of evangelism. When Jesus appears to his disciples after his resurrection, he tells them that they are to be his witnesses in Jerusalem, and in all Judea and Samaria, and to the ends of the earth (Acts 1:8). Paul refers to this responsibility of believers as the "ministry of reconciliation":

> Therefore, if anyone is in Christ, he is a new creation; the old has gone, the new has come! All this is from God, who reconciled us to himself through Christ and gave us the ministry of reconciliation: that God was reconciling the world to himself in

Christ, not counting men's sins against them. And *he has committed to us the message of reconciliation. We are therefore Christ's ambassadors, as though God were making his appeal through us.* (2 Cor. 5:17–20)

This ministry of reconciliation, this responsibility to communicate the message of the good news of Jesus Christ, belongs to *every* believer, not just to those who have been specially gifted or set apart for the task. Here again it should inspire us in our evangelistic efforts to realize that every time we muster the courage to speak to a friend or neighbor about the gospel, we are demonstrating our spiritual genetic link with all of the Old Testament prophets who at times seem so distant, as well as manifesting in our lives the Spirit's work of conforming us to the likeness of Christ, the Word of God.

Of course, ambassadors do not just represent their heads of state with words. We should expect, therefore, that "Christ's ambassadors" also have a representative responsibility that extends beyond the verbal realm. Communicating the truth about God—representing him fully, being his ambassador—also involves our actions. This is an area of Christian representational responsibility that has received far less attention in the church than has the verbal aspect, yet it is an absolutely vital component of our prophetic task. If the church is to carry out its prophetic responsibility fully and effectively, how we should represent God behaviorally is a necessary consideration.

Behaviorally

It may come as a bit of a surprise to learn that many passages in the Scriptures talk about Christian *behavior* in the context of communicating the truth about God. For example, in his Sermon on the Mount, Jesus tells his disciples to "let your light shine before men, *that they may see your good deeds* and praise your Father in heaven" (Matt. 5:16). Evidently, then, our deeds, our actions, our behaviors, are meant to be seen and to reveal to those who see them something praiseworthy about God. Jesus' words are echoed by the apostle Peter, when he writes that the people of God are to "live such good lives among the pagans that, though they accuse you of doing wrong, they *may see your good deeds* and glorify God on the day he visits us" (1 Peter 2:12).[10] Gene Getz is absolutely correct in his insistence that this behavioral aspect of our Christian witness is not some sort of welcome, but unnecessary adjunct to the verbal aspect, but an essential complement to it, giving substance and visible expression to our words:

> The body of Christ is . . . God's divine means for getting beyond the verbalization level in our Christian witness. It is as non-Christians *see* the body functioning in *love* and *unity* that they become convinced of the reality of Christianity. Once again it must be emphasized that this becomes the experiential backdrop against which "words *about* Jesus Christ" take on meaning and true significance. McLuhan's phrase then, "the medium is the message," is actually a biblical concept. It is the *medium* (the body of Christ) that actually *becomes* the message to the unsaved world.[11]

Affectively

Just as the prophets of the Old Testament, contemporary believers are called upon to represent God with all aspects

---

10. See also 1 Peter 3:13–16; 1 Thess. 4:11–12.

11. Getz, *Sharpening the Focus of the Church,* 184–85.

of their beings, including those affective dimensions of our being closely associated with our emotions. We are commanded to demonstrate compassion (Col. 3:12–14), forgiveness (Matt. 6:12; Eph. 4:32; Col. 3:12–14), love (John 13:34–35), and joy (John 17:13), for example, not just because these are characteristics of the fully realized humanity that God intends for us to experience, but also because exercising these affective behaviors toward one another and unbelievers demonstrates dimensions of God's own personality. Jesus says, "As I have loved you, so you must love one another" (John 13:34). When we exercise this love toward one another, we are demonstrating a truth about God; that is, that he is a loving being.

Emotions are often left to run where they will without any thought about the important role they also have to play in our Christian witness. Worse yet, sometimes we allow emotions to be the driving force behind our actions. If we feel a certain way about someone or something, we allow that feeling to control our thoughts, and subsequently our actions. Many disagreements, fights, and even splits in the church have come about by this process. Instead of allowing our renewed minds (Rom. 12:1–2) to govern our actions, resulting in appropriate emotions, we flip this around so that emotions govern our minds, affecting what we do. Once we realize, however, that this emotional part of our being is also called to witness prophetically to the truth about God, we will begin consciously to take control of our emotions and make them serve us (and God), rather than the other way around.

Completely
We have been considering our representational responsibilities in isolation, but of course they never occur in isolation in real life. Words, actions, and emotions all exist in an

interactive complex in each individual. We must be careful to ensure that the message that each of these aspects of our beings communicates to those around us does not contradict the message communicated by any other aspect. That is, all aspects of our beings must be communicating the same thing; they must be in harmony. For the church to be effective in her witness, we must first recognize and acknowledge our representative responsibility and then set about the difficult challenge of representing God with our entire beings, both individually and corporately as the community of God's people.[12]

There has been an overemphasis on the verbal dimension of our witness in the world to the neglect of the other representational aspects, but this is contrary to the commands and examples of Scripture.[13] The apostle Paul, describing his own representation of God with his entire being, says: "I will not venture to speak of anything except what Christ has accomplished through me in leading the Gentiles to obey God by what I have said *and done*" (Rom. 15:18). Yes, there was certainly a verbal component to Paul's message, but this was complemented by a behavioral component that did not contradict it. In his exhortation to the church at

12. E. Clinton Gardner, *The Church as a Prophetic Community* (Philadelphia: Westminster, 1967), 180: "Seen in the light of the radical monotheism of Biblical faith and the New Testament conception of koinonia, the church is in its very nature a prophetic community. It exists in the world, but its purpose is to point men to God, the true center of their existence and the ultimate ground of meaning and value."

13. Snyder, *Community of the King*, 101, n. 2, citing Michael Green, *Evangelism in the Early Church* (Grand Rapids: Eerdmans, 1970), 48: "There has been undue concentration on what has become technically known as the 'Kerygma,' which is supposed to have been a fairly fixed body of preaching material common to the early missionaries. . . . In the New Testament the root *kērussein* (to 'proclaim') is by no means primary. It is just one of the three great words used to refer to the proclaiming of the Christian message, the other two being *euaggelizesthai* (to 'tell the good news') and *marturein* (to 'bear witness')."

Philippi, Paul warns against such contradiction: "Whatever happens, *conduct yourselves* in a manner worthy of the gospel of Christ" (Phil. 1:27). He later commands them to lead lives of such faultless and shining behavior that they would stand out against the blackness of sin as they hold out the word of life (Phil. 2:14–16). That is, their behavior (and ours) should substantiate the accompanying words so that the words are not discounted. In fact, Paul warns Titus, his son in the faith, against those in whom the contradiction between words and actions was all too apparent. His criticism of such people is scathing: "They claim to know God, but by their actions they deny him. They are detestable, disobedient and unfit for doing anything good" (Titus 1:16). Gene Getz summarizes the biblical mandate to maintain continuity between our words and behaviors: "Communication [here he means strictly verbal communication] must be solidly aligned with a Christian life style—both at the individual and corporate level. This Christian life style must be demonstrated in the various contexts of living—the Christian's business life, his social life, his home life, his church life, and his life in general."[14]

We, as the people of God, must come to grips with the fact that we are prophetically called to make our entire beings increasingly accurate representations of God. Although this may at first appear beyond our capabilities, we must remember that from the very beginning of time it has been the task of humankind to bear the image of God (Gen. 1:26). Simply stated, we, as redeemed humanity, should be about the business of doing what we were created to do. In fulfilling our function, we are both fulfilling a prophetic task and evangelistically communicating the truth about God to onlooking unbelievers. Thus, Howard Snyder is correct in his

14. Getz, *Sharpening the Focus of the Church*, 36.

conclusion that "the Church is called to be prophetically evangelistic and evangelistically prophetic."[15]

Once we realize the enormity of the task to which we have been called, we may understandably be tempted to shrink back with a sense of inadequacy. However, God has equipped us for the task. The apostle Peter informs us, "His divine power has given us everything we need for life and godliness through our knowledge of him who called us by his own glory and goodness" (2 Peter 1:3). We venture forth to fulfill our daunting task of representing God with full knowledge of our utter dependence upon him and need to draw from the strength that he provides.

Even after accepting this enormous responsibility, however, our prophetic work is not yet finished. To fulfill the prophetic task we must also represent the community of which we are a part. Just as Israel represented the community of nations of which she was a member, so too the church must represent the entirety of humanity of which she is only a part. We can take our cues from Israel regarding how we should carry out this particular dimension of our representative responsibility.

THE CHURCH MUST REPRESENT HUMANITY

When we pause to reflect on exactly what it means for the church to represent humanity, we must first clarify what we mean by "humanity." Just whom is the church supposed to represent? As we have seen in chapter 4, the nation of Is-

---

15. Snyder, *Community of the King*, 99. Robert Lewis and Rob Wilkins, *The Church of the Irresistible Influence* (Grand Rapids: Zondervan, 2001), 41, similarly maintain that one of the central functions of the church is to "present living proof of a loving God to a watching world."

FIGURE 3
The Prophetic Character of the People of God

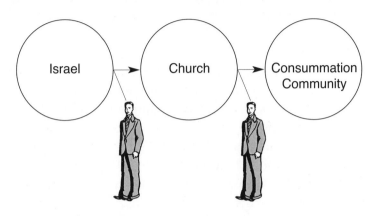

rael, as it is presented in the Old Testament, pointed forward prophetically to the New Covenant community that God would gather to himself by means of the redemptive work of Christ. In other words, Israel prophetically represented the church. Looking back on the scriptural accounts of Israel, we see enacted in actual history (that is, prophetically represented behaviorally) the broad strokes of God's redemptive activity in Jesus Christ. Therefore, it is reasonable and necessary to conclude that the covenant community that Israel typified also has a prophetic responsibility to represent a future community. This community can be nothing other than the purified, post-judgment inhabitants of the new heaven and the new earth. This is illustrated in figure 3.

This divinely orchestrated prophetic representation, in which at each stage of redemptive history the people of God typologically represent the next stage, was recognized very early in the church. For example, Origen (ca. 185–255) understood that "just as the Old Testament is a shadow of the New, the New Testament in turn is a shadow of the kingdom to come."[16] It is with a self-awareness of the church's place and purpose in this ongoing process that we consider what it means, in practical terms, for us to represent humanity.

Verbally

The church must be self-conscious in its representational use of words. In the Scriptures, we are given both examples and exhortations concerning the use of words. The first representational use of words is one we have seen before—intercessory prayer. We are told to be faithful in prayer (Rom. 12:12) and to pray continually (1 Thess. 5:17). Prayer is part of the Christian's armor (Eph. 6:18). Included among those for whom this prayer is to be offered are those outside the community of faith—even those who persecute us (Matt. 5:44).

There is another representational use of words, however. Just as the community of Israel prophetically pointed forward to the church (which comprises all nations), so also the church prophetically points forward to the purified community of the new heavens and new earth. The church, in the present, is to demonstrate to unbelievers what humanity should, and was intended to, look like; in other words, what the consummation community *will* look like. We are to demonstrate a reality in which unbelievers are invited to participate and to which the gospel calls them. In this redeemed humanity, words build up and correct out of love. Thus we find commands for mutual exhortation (1 Tim. 5:1), encouragement (2 Tim. 4:2; Titus 2:15; Heb. 10:24–25), correction (2 Tim. 4:2), and rebuke (1 Tim. 5:20; 2 Tim. 4:2; Titus 1:13; 2:15). These commands are summarized in a

---

16. Daniélou, *Origen*, 171. See also Miroslav Volf, "The Church as a Prophetic Community and a Sign of Hope," *EuroJTh* 2/1 (1993): 16: "The historical life of the church should image its eschatological future in the new creation."

general command for all of our conversation to be edifying: "Do not let any unwholesome talk come out of your mouths, but only what is helpful for building others up according to their needs, that it may benefit those who listen" (Eph. 4:29).

Speaking, however, is only one small part of human behavior. Our conversation in the broader, older sense of "the manner of conducting oneself in the world or in society; behavior, mode or course of life"[17] also has prophetic implications.

Behaviorally

This demonstration of what God intended humanity to be also extends to our behavior. As a result of sin, human beings have discord, strife, self-centeredness, and all the other problems associated with personal and communal fragmentation. In contrast to this, the church is called to represent a true humanity in which each member belongs to all the others (Rom.12:4; 1 Cor. 12:24–27), in which we are united in God and look to the concerns and interests of others (Phil. 2:1–5). In short, the church is to demonstrate to a fractured and fractious humanity the humanity God intended.

Fulfilling our prophetic responsibility to represent behaviorally a healed humanity is absolutely critical for the effectiveness of the verbal message of good news. Howard Snyder puts it well:

> Pragmatically it is self-evident that there can be no procedure of proclamation without a community, distinct from the rest of society, to do the proclaiming. Pragmatically it is just as clear that there can be no evangelistic call addressed to a person inviting

---

17. *The Compact Oxford English Dictionary*, 330.

him to enter into a new kind of fellowship and learning if there is not such a body of persons, again distinct
from the totality of society, to whom he can come and
with whom he can learn. . . . If it is not the case that
there are in a given place men of various characters
and origins who have been brought together in Jesus
Christ, then there is not in that place the new humanity and in that place the gospel is not true. If, on the
other hand, this miracle of new creation has occurred,
then all the verbalizations and interpretations whereby
this brotherhood communicates to the world around it
are simply explications of the fact of its presence.[18]

Snyder is saying that it makes no sense to call people to en-
joy a new humanity when there is no evidence of that new
humanity for them to see. When we come to realize that
everything we do as a local congregation has prophetic implications, we will evaluate seriously not only everything we
do, but also how we do those things. We will carry out our
programs, activities, and all the other initiatives of the church
with new health and vigor because we will do them with an
eye toward how they are perceived by unbelieving onlookers
(that is, how they are fulfilling the prophetic behavioral representative function) instead of, as is more often the case,
whether they are satisfying the felt needs of the participants.

Affectively

The new humanity that the church demonstrates also
has its affective dimension, and the Bible is not silent on this

---

18. Snyder, *Community of the King*, 73–74, citing John Howard Yoder, "A People
in the World: Theological Interpretation," in *The Concept of the Believers' Church*, ed.
James L. Garrett Jr. (Scottdale, Pa.: Herald, 1967), 259. Lewis and Wilkins, *The
Church of the Irresistible Influence*, 48, state the principle more simply: "What the world
waits to see is whether what we [the church] have is better than what they have."

aspect of its nature. We are told that in this new humanity, we should share in the feelings of our brothers and sisters (Rom. 12:15). Also, contrary to those in rebellion against God, even our mourning is not without hope (1 Thess. 4:13). Even the worst circumstances are not able to rob us of the joy that is ours in Christ (1 Thess. 5:16).

However, it is difficult these days to harness our emotions and bring them into the service of God because so much in our society promotes emotions as the determining force in our lives. We are told to do things if "it feels good," to buy things that make us happy, to leave commitments that don't excite us, to change churches if our "felt needs" aren't being met. The difference between these cultural recommendations and the biblical pattern is simply that the former would have us focus on ourselves while God would have us focus on others. If an unbeliever looks at a local congregation and sees that personal emotions dictate the actions of its members, what is there that is different from his own situation that would attract him? In the church, even our emotions demonstrate the new humanity when we are more affected by the circumstances of others than by our own. Hunger drives, service projects, day-care, literacy programs, job placement assistance, and other efforts by local congregations communicate something of the properly oriented affections of the new humanity the church is supposed to model.

THE CHURCH'S REPRESENTATIONAL FUNCTIONS COALESCE

The church, therefore, is responsible not only to represent God, but also to represent to unbelievers the new humanity available to them through Christ. As the church carries out her prophetic tasks better and better, however, it

becomes increasingly difficult to separate these representational responsibilities. Since humanity was created to bear
the image of God, then representing true humanity is all
about representing God. One of the primary ways believers
demonstrate true humanity and God at the same time is by
their unity. The unity of believers demonstrates the unity of
God and the unity intended for humanity. In his prayer for
believers, Jesus himself makes this point:

> My prayer is not for them alone. I pray also for those
> who will believe in me through their message, that all
> of them may be one, Father, just as you are in me
> and I am in you. May they also be in us so that the
> world may believe that you have sent me. I have
> given them the glory that you gave me, that they may
> be one as we are one: I in them and you in me. May
> they be brought to complete unity to let the world
> know that you sent me and have loved them even as
> you have loved me. (John 17:20–23)[19]

The church has the prophetic responsibility to communicate verbally, behaviorally, and affectively what God
is like and what humanity can be. The apostle Paul de-
lights to see the Corinthian church carrying out this task
well. He commends them: "You yourselves are our letter,
written on our hearts, *known and read by everybody*. You
know that you are a letter from Christ, the result of our
ministry, written not with ink but with the Spirit of the living God, not on tablets of stone but on tablets of human
hearts" (2 Cor. 3:2–3).

---

19. See also 1 Cor. 1:10–17. Snyder, *Community of the King,* 171: "The fact that
God is one provides the foundation for the New Testament emphasis on the unity
of the gospel and of the Church."

THE SPECIAL RESPONSIBILITY OF
CHURCH LEADERS

While it is true that every member of the church bears
the responsibility of carrying out the prophetic functions described in this chapter, it falls upon church leaders to demonstrate how this is done. Church leaders must set an example
of modeling Christ and redeemed humanity; that is, they
must model modeling. Thus we read Paul saying, "Follow my
example, as I follow the example of Christ" (1 Cor. 11:1);
and, "Whatever you have learned or received or heard from
me, *or seen in me*—put it into practice" (Phil. 4:9). He commands a similar type of imitable example from Timothy:

> Command and teach these things. Don't let anyone
> look down on you because you are young, but *set an
> example* for the believers in speech, in life, in love, in
> faith and in purity. . . . Be diligent in these matters;
> give yourself wholly to them, *so that everyone may see*
> your progress. Watch *your life* and your doctrine
> closely. Persevere in them, because if you do, you will
> save both yourself and your hearers. (1 Tim.
> 4:11–16)

In their book dealing with the responsibilities of church
leaders, Larry Richards and Clyde Hoeldtke similarly discuss the heavier responsibility of leaders to teach with their
lives the truths they speak:

> All too often we attempt to communicate the written
> Word only in verbal form. And we are amazed when
> so many believers fail to make the choice to obey the
> Word and put it into practice. But the error is ours.
> For verbal communication is to be accompanied by

a lifestyle demonstration of the realities taught. When the Word is taught *and* lived by the spiritual leader, the responsiveness comes and choices to obey are made. . . .

The Christian both hears the Word from his spiritual leader and sees the Word expressed in his person. The open life of leaders among—not over—the brothers and sisters is a revelation of the very face of Jesus. And to see Jesus expressing Himself in a human being brings the hope that transformation might be a possibility for me too.[20]

So, while the church as a whole is called to carry out the prophetic tasks of representing both God and humanity in the ways we have described, the leaders have the additional responsibility of demonstrating how to do this. In this connection, it is instructive to note that the biblical qualifications for church leaders are almost exclusively behavioral. First Timothy 3:1–13 and Titus 1:6–9 require that a leader in the church be hospitable, gentle, not quarrelsome, not a lover of money, not a recent convert, one who has a good reputation with outsiders, not overbearing, not quick-tempered, one who loves what is good, upright, disciplined, above reproach, monogamous, temperate, respectable, not given to drunkenness, one who manages his own household well, one whose children obey him, not one who pursues dishonest gain, one who keeps hold of the deep truths, sincere, and tested. The only qualification that is of a more verbal nature is the requirement that the leader be able to teach (1 Tim. 3:2; 5:17; Titus 1:9). How often we stress the verbal competencies in our leaders to a much greater degree than their

20. Lawrence O. Richards and Clyde Hoeldtke, *Church Leadership: Following the Example of Jesus Christ* (Grand Rapids: Zondervan, 1980), 116, 120.

behavior! What we must grow to appreciate more fully is that the behavior of our leaders speaks a more full-bodied message to us and the unbelieving world than do their occasional homilies—whether for good or for ill. A simple realization of this fact will go a long way toward enhancing the witness of the church in the contemporary world.

CONCLUSION

We have seen that the church can trace her spiritual DNA back to the prophets of the Old Testament. Like them, she has been called by God to undertake a task that requires nothing less than the involvement of every area of her life. There can be no such thing as a separation of our "church life" and our "real life," for our "church life" demands whole-life participation in our prophetic vocation. As the charismatic *community* of the people of *God,* the church is called to demonstrate what an ideal human community should look like and, even more challenging, what God is like. This monumental assignment requires the enlistment of every area of our beings: our words, our actions, and even our affections. Nothing about us is exempt from this call to service.

There are two important points to keep in mind as we reflect on the church's engagement in its prophetic vocation. First, the verbal, behavioral, and affective dimensions of our prophetic representation must be in alignment, so that they do not contradict each other. Our words must be corroborated by our actions, and our affections must give genuine expression to both. Hypocrisy is very easy to detect and is perhaps the biggest stumbling block, or excuse, for unbelievers and, therefore, the biggest deterrent to the effectiveness of the church's prophetic witness in the world.

Second, the church cannot overemphasize the verbal, behavioral, or affective dimension of our prophetic witness without presenting a faulty picture of God and of the ideal humanity we are responsible to represent. It is very likely that every one of us has experienced local congregations in which one of these areas was stressed at the expense of the others. Such overemphases result in churches with wonderful doctrine but no comparably wonderful practice, churches with fantastic social engagement that appears to come at the expense of truth, and churches with such an emphasis on emotion that doctrine and practice seem to melt away into irrelevance. It is our task not only to ensure that the church prophetically represents God and humanity verbally, behaviorally, and affectively, but also to ensure that the words, actions, and emotions are integrated and in balance.

The church's prophetic task is enormous and extremely difficult. It is no wonder that so many of the Old Testament prophets objected to their prophetic call. Yet the divine assurance they received has also been given to us: "Surely I am with you always, to the very end of the age" (Matt. 28:20). The Spirit of the perfect prophet, the Holy Spirit, indwells every believer and provides us with the understanding, the resources, and the power to fulfill our prophetic calling. As the church depends upon God, she will see the course laid out before her and successfully travel it to its blessed end.

FOR FURTHER REFLECTION

1. Reflect on how your understanding of what a local church should be has affected the way you have participated in the mission of the larger, universal church.

2. What areas of the prophetic task do you believe your local church does particularly well, and in what areas do you think it needs to improve? What steps could you take toward making this happen?

3. Consider your own congregation in light of your understanding of the prophetic task. What does your community of faith nonverbally communicate about the gospel to unbelieving visitors or others in the neighborhood?

4. List one specific function that your church carries out for each of the areas of prophetic responsibility.

5. How might a specific outreach effort in your church be enhanced by a fuller understanding of the multifaceted prophetic task? Describe what this might look like.

CONCLUDING
REMARKS

We have traveled a fascinating investigative journey together, in which we have observed the multifaceted activities of this remarkable biblical figure called a prophet. Perhaps the simplest way to summarize the different dimensions of our discoveries is by means of an illustration. Figure 4 represents the types of the Old Testament on the left side with their antitypes on the right.

FIGURE 4
The Realization of Old Testament Types

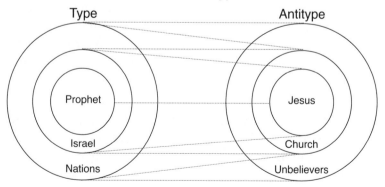

It seems a picture is worth *at least* a thousand words. Although this diagram appears at first glance to be almost incomprehensible with its circles, labels, and dotted lines, it effectively encapsulates the different stages of our journey of discovery. The circle surrounding PROPHET represents chapters 1 and 2, in which we examined more closely the question of what exactly a prophet is supposed to be. The relationship between the PROPHET circle and the ISRAEL circle was considered in chapter 3, where we investigated what a prophet does and how he does it. In chapter 4 we discussed Israel's prophetic function, which, paralleling the individual prophet's function, is represented by the relationship between the ISRAEL circle and the NATIONS circle. That these Old Testament realities are also types of later redemptive realities is indicated by the right side of the diagram and the dotted lines that connect it to the left side. The prophet finds his ultimate fulfillment in the perfect prophet, Jesus Christ. The nation of Israel too finds the focus of its prophetic task among the nations in Christ. Chapter 5, where we discussed Jesus' prophetic role, extensively detailed these connections. Just as Israel had a prophetic function to carry out in the community of nations of which she was a constituent member, so also the church, the redeemed community of God comprising representatives from those nations and others, has a prophetic function to carry out for the unbelievers among whom she currently finds herself. It was the goal of chapter 6 to elucidate these prophetic responsibilities and provide some direction for their faithful execution.

Contrary to most books that suggest new directions, programs, or visions for the church, the purpose of this study has been to lay out the direction, program, and vision that the church has already been provided by means of its calling as a prophetic people. Whenever a new idea is promoted in the church, we, by reflecting on what a prophetic agent is (whether an individual or community) and what that agent is supposed to do, will be in a secure position from which to evaluate not only the legitimacy of the proposed idea in terms of its compatibility with the prophetic nature of the church, but also, at least to some extent, its content. If, for example, an inner-city church decides to contour its programs to focus exclusively on urgent social concerns, we recognize because of our examination of the prophets that this effort, though important and not to be neglected, is only a fraction of the prophetic responsibilities that should characterize the people of God, who strive to represent not only what humanity is intended to be, but also the full redemptive message of God to their community. Similarly, if a suburban church decides (consciously or unconsciously) to focus exclusively on delivering the message of salvation to its community (and usually only verbally when done at all), it is neglecting the dimension of prophetic responsibility that calls for representing to the community a humanity interrelating in a way that demonstrates the reconciliation that God provides even at our interpersonal level.

Reflection on the nature and function of a prophet gives a coherent focus to every individual church's self-perception and provides meaningful direction to every activity in which it engages.[1] Understanding the multifaceted responsibilities of the prophetic calling will safeguard us against overemphasizing or neglecting any individual prophetic function,

1. In the words of Arnold B. Rhodes, "Israel's Prophets as Intercessors," in *Scripture and Theology: Essays in Honor of J. Coert Rylaarsdam*, ed. Arthur L. Merrill and Thomas W. Overholt (Pittsburgh: Pickwick, 1977), 108: "It is crucial that no aspect of the ministry of Israel's prophets be overlooked in establishing valid criteria for determining the nature of 'prophetic ministry' in the present-day covenant community and the contemporary world. There is a need to appreciate Israel's prophets in the fullness of their faith and life."

and the church will more accurately reflect God and a humanity effectively bearing his image.

During those rare occasions when we read the books of the prophets of the Old Testament (or rarer still, when we hear a sermon about one), we probably have one of two basic reactions. We may begin to tune out because we have decided that these Old Testament characters have little to do with our world of Big Macs, DVDs, and the Internet. After all, what could a two- or three-thousand-year-old prophet have to say to me? Surely I lose nothing by focusing exclusively on the New Testament. Another possible reaction is almost the opposite. We may consider the characters that we encounter in the pages of the prophetic texts so grand and glorious, carrying out their prophetic tasks usually in the face of tremendous opposition, that we may conclude that they are far beyond our ability to imitate. Surely these characters are to be admired, but they are almost mythical in their courage and faithfulness. We may understandably conclude that we could never do what they did.

We are, however, called to do exactly that. Our spiritual ancestors have shown us what to do and how to do it. Moreover, we have been assured of divine assistance to carry out our task. Once we really come to grips with the facts that we are the direct heirs of the prophetic mantle borne by the likes of Isaiah, Jeremiah, and Ezekiel, that we are the redemptive focus of Israel's entire typical existence, and that we are the physical expressions of the living God, our participation in the local church cannot fail to take on a wonderful, expansive, and energizing significance.

We may hesitate to accept what may seem to be an overwhelming responsibility, but there is no need to fear. We have the opportunity with every word we say, every action we perform, and every emotion we express in the course of our everyday lives to be about the prophetic task. We have seen how our Lord brought all of the aspects of the office of prophet into the sharpest focus in himself. It is now the time for each one of us, being conformed to his likeness, to fulfill the prophetic task for which we have been called. May we do so with understanding and enthusiasm wedded together to produce an effective, dynamic witness to those who have eyes to see and ears to hear.

SOURCES
CONSULTED

Abbott-Smith, G. *A Manual Greek Lexicon of the New Testament*. Edinburgh: T. & T. Clark, 1981.

Aigbee, Sunday. "A Biblical Foundation for the Prophetic Mandate." *Pneuma* 11/2 (1989): 77–98.

Albright, William F. *From the Stone Age to Christianity*. Garden City, N.Y.: Doubleday, 1957.

Allender, Dan. "Mimicking Our Disruptive Father and Our Diverse Older Brother." *Mars Hill Review* 5 (1996): 35–46.

Aquinas, Thomas. *Summa Theologica*. 5 vols. Translated by Fathers of the English Dominican Province. Westminster, Md.: Christian Classics, 1981.

Bailey, Lloyd R. "The Prophetic Critique of Israel's Cultic Order." *Faith and Mission* 6/2 (1989): 41–57.

Balentine, Samuel E. "The Prophet as Intercessor: A Reassessment." *JBL* 103/2 (1984): 161–73.

Barker, Kenneth, ed. *The NIV Study Bible: New International Version*. Grand Rapids: Zondervan, 1985.

Berkhof, Louis. *Introduction to Systematic Theology*. Grand Rapids: Baker, 1979, reprint.

————. *Principles of Biblical Interpretation*. Grand Rapids: Baker, 1950.

————. *Systematic Theology*. 4th ed. Grand Rapids: Eerdmans, 1941.

Blenkinsopp, J. *A History of Prophecy in Israel*. Philadelphia: Westminster, 1983.

Boadt, Lawrence. *The Hebrew Prophets: Visionaries of the Ancient World*. New York: St. Martin's Griffin, 1997.

Botterweck, G. Johannes, Helmer Ringgren, and Heinz-Josef Fabry. *Theological Dictionary of the Old Testament*. 12 vols. to date. Translated by Douglas W. Stott et al. Grand Rapids: Eerdmans, 1974–.

Breck, John. *The Power of the Word: In the Worshipping Church*. Crestwood, N.Y.: St. Vladimir's Seminary, 1986.

Buttrick, George A., et al., eds. *The Interpreter's Dictionary of the Bible*. 4 vols. Nashville: Abingdon, 1962.

Calvin, John. *Commentaries on the Epistle of Paul the Apostle to the Hebrews*. Translated by John Owen. Grand Rapids: Baker, 1996 reprint.

————. *Institutes of the Christian Religion*. Edited by John T. McNeill. Translated by Ford Lewis Battles. Philadelphia: Westminster, 1960.

Carroll, Robert P. *From Chaos to Covenant: Prophecy in the Book of Jeremiah*. New York: Crossroad, 1981.

Castell, Alburey and Donald M. Borchert. *An Introduction to Modern Philosophy: Examining the Human Condition*. New York: Macmillan, 1983.

Charity, A. C. *Events and Their Afterlife: The Dialectics of Christian Typology in the Bible and Dante*. Cambridge: Cambridge University Press, 1966.

Charles, R. H. *A Critical and Exegetical Commentary on the Book of Daniel*. Oxford: Clarendon, 1929.

Clements, R. E. "The Purpose of the Book of Jonah." VTSup 28 (1974): 16–28.

The Compact Oxford English Dictionary. 2d ed. Oxford: Clarendon, 1991.

Conlon, Steve. "The Art of Adventure Travel. In the 1990–91 catalog of the Above the Clouds Trekking Agency (P.O. Box 398, Worcester, MA 01602), p. 2. Cited by David Zurick, *Errant Journeys,* 135–36. Austin: University of Texas Press, 1995.

Corbett, J. Elliot, and Elizabeth S. Smith. *Becoming a Prophetic Community.* Atlanta: John Knox, 1980.

Costas, Orlando E. *The Church and Its Mission: A Shattering Critique from the Third World.* Wheaton, Ill.: Tyndale, 1974.

Crim, Keith, et al., eds. *Interpreter's Dictionary of the Bible: Supplementary Volume.* Nashville: Abingdon, 1976.

Cross, Frank M. *Canaanite Myth and Hebrew Epic.* Cambridge: Harvard University Press, 1973.

Crouzel, Henri. *Origen.* Translated by A. S. Worrall. San Francisco: Harper and Row, 1989.

Daniélou, Jean. *From Shadows to Reality: Studies in the Biblical Typology of the Fathers.* Translated by Dom Wulstan Hibberd. Westminster: Newman, 1960.

———. *Origen.* Translated by Walter Mitchell. New York: Sheed and Ward, 1955.

DeVries, Simon. *Prophet Against Prophet: The Role of the Micaiah Narrative (1 Kings 22) in the Development of Early Prophetic Tradition.* Grand Rapids: Eerdmans, 1978.

Dörries, Hermann, "The Prophetical Ministry of the Church." *The Lutheran Quarterly* 1/4 (1949): 363–68.

Doyle, Sir Arthur Conan. *The Complete Sherlock Holmes.* Garden City, N.Y.: Doubleday, 1930.

Duhm, Bernhard. *Das Buch Jesaja.* Göttingen: Vandenhoeck & Ruprecht, 1982 reprint.

Elwell, Walter A., ed. *Evangelical Dictionary of Theology.* Grand Rapids: Baker, 1984.

Evans, Mary. *Prophets of the Lord.* London: Paternoster, 1992.

Fairbairn, Patrick. *The Typology of Scripture: Viewed in Connection with the Whole Series of the Divine Dispensations.* 2 vols. Grand Rapids: Baker, 1975 reprint.

Freedman, David Noel. "Between God and Man: Prophets in Ancient Israel." In *Prophecy and Prophets,* edited by Yehoshua Gitay, 57–87. Atlanta: Scholars, 1997.

Freeman, Hobart E. *An Introduction to the Old Testament Prophets.* Chicago: Moody, 1968.

Friebel, Kelvin G. *Jeremiah's and Ezekiel's Sign-Acts: Rhetorical Non-verbal Communication.* JSOTSup 283. Sheffield: Sheffield Academic Press, 1999.

Galbraith, John P. "The World's Need for a Prophetic Church." In *Prophetic Witness in a Bewildered World,* 3–15. Nîmes: Reformed Ecumenical Synod Missions Conference, 1980.

Gardner, E. Clinton. *The Church as a Prophetic Community.* Philadelphia: Westminster, 1967.

Garner, Bryan A., ed. *Black's Law Dictionary.* St. Paul: West Group, 1999.

Gelb, Ignace J., et al., eds. *The Assyrian Dictionary of the Oriental Institute of the University of Chicago.* Chicago: Oriental Institute, 1956–.

Gesenius, William. *A Hebrew and English Lexicon of the Old Testament.* 3d ed. Translated by Edward Robinson. Boston: Crocker & Brewster, 1849.

Getz, Gene A. *Sharpening the Focus of the Church.* Chicago: Moody, 1974.

Gill, Robin. "Prophecy in a Socially Determined Church." *Theology* 82 (1979): 24–30.

Gitay, Yehoshua. *Prophecy and Prophets: The Diversity of Contemporary Issues in Scholarship.* Society of Biblical Literature. Semeia Series. Atlanta: Scholars, 1997.

Goldingay, John. *Models for Interpretation of Scripture*. Grand Rapids: Eerdmans, 1995.

Goppelt, Leonhard. *Typos: The Typological Interpretation of the Old Testament in the New*. Translated by Donald H. Madvig. Grand Rapids: Eerdmans, 1982.

Gordon, Robert P., ed. *The Place Is Too Small for Us: The Israelite Prophets in Recent Scholarship*. Winona Lake, Ind.: Eisenbrauns, 1995.

Grabbe, Lester L. *Priests, Prophets, Diviners, Sages: A Socio-Historical Study of Religious Specialists in Ancient Israel*. Valley Forge, Pa.: Trinity, 1995.

Greidanus, Sidney. *Preaching Christ from the Old Testament: A Contemporary Hermeneutical Method*. Grand Rapids: Eerdmans, 1999.

Grottanelli, Cristiano. *Kings and Prophets: Monarchic Power, Inspired Leadership, and Sacred Text in Biblical Narrative*. Oxford: Oxford University Press, 1999.

Grudem, Wayne. *Systematic Theology: An Introduction to Biblical Doctrine*. Grand Rapids: Zondervan, 1994.

Gunkel, Hermann. "Die geheimen Erfahrungen der Propheten Israels." *Suchen der Zeit* 1 (1903): 112–53.

Habel, N. "The Form and Significance of the Call Narratives." *ZAW* 77 (1965): 297–323.

Hamerton-Kelly, Robert G. *The Divine Passion: Reflections on the Prophets*. Nashville: The Upper Room, 1988.

Heaton, E. W. *The Old Testament Prophets*. Atlanta: John Knox, 1977.

Herion, Gary. "The Impact of Modern and Social Science Assumptions on the Reconstruction of Israelite History." *JSOT* 34 (1986): 3–33.

Heschel, Abraham J. *The Prophets*. New York: Harper & Row, 1962.

Hölscher, G. *Die Propheten: Untersuchungen zur Religionsgeschichte Israels*. Leipzig: J. Hinrichs, 1914.

Holwerda, David E. *Jesus and Israel: One Covenant or Two?* Grand Rapids: Eerdmans, 1995.

Jenni, Ernst, and Claus Westermann. *Theological Lexicon of the Old Testament*. 3 vols. Translated by Mark E. Biddle. Peabody, Mass.: Hendrickson, 1997.

Johnson, Aubrey R. *The Cultic Prophet in Ancient Israel*. 2d ed. Cardiff: University of Wales Press, 1962.

Kaiser, Walter C., and Moisés Silva. *An Introduction to Biblical Hermeneutics: The Search for Meaning*. Grand Rapids: Zondervan, 1994.

Koch, Klaus. *The Growth of the Biblical Tradition: The Form-Critical Method*. New York: Macmillan, 1969.

———. *The Prophets*. Vol. 1: *The Assyrian Period*. Translated by Margaret Kohl. Philadelphia: Fortress, 1982.

König, Adrio. "The Prophetic Witness of the Church." In *Prophetic Witness in a Bewildered World*, 17–46. Nîmes: Reformed Ecumenical Synod Missions Conference, 1980.

Landis, Benson Y. *A Rauschenbusch Reader: The Kingdom of God and the Social Gospel*. New York: Harper & Brothers, 1957.

LaRondelle, Hans K. *The Israel of God in Prophecy: Principles of Prophetic Interpretation*. Berrien Springs, Mich.: Andrews University Press, 1983.

Lewis, Robert, and Rob Wilkins. *The Church of the Irresistible Influence*. Grand Rapids: Zondervan, 2001.

Lindblom, Johannes. *Prophecy in Ancient Israel*. Philadelphia: Fortress, 1962.

Lindsey, Hal. *The Late Great Planet Earth*. Grand Rapids: Zondervan, 1970.

Longman, Tremper, III. *Immanuel in Our Place: Seeing Christ in Israel's Worship*. Phillipsburg, N.J.: P&R, 2001.

———. *Reading the Bible with Heart and Mind*. Colorado Springs: NavPress, 1997.

Lowry, David. *The Prophetic Element in the Church: As Conceived in the Theology of Karl Rahner.* Lanham, Md.: University Press of America, 1990.

Mataboge, Ezekiel M. "The Prophetic Witness of the Church: A Response." In *Prophetic Witness in a Bewildered World,* 43–46. Nîmes: Reformed Ecumenical Synod Missions Conference, 1980.

Mays, James Luther, and Paul J. Achtemeier, eds. *Interpreting the Prophets.* Philadelphia: Fortress, 1987.

McConville, J. G. *Judgment and Promise: An Interpretation of the Book of Jeremiah.* Winona Lake, Ind.: Eisenbrauns, 1993.

Miller, John W. *Meet the Prophets: A Beginner's Guide to the Books of the Biblical Prophets—Their Meaning Then and Now.* New York: Paulist, 1987.

Miller, Patrick D., Jr. " 'Moses My Servant': The Deuteronomic Portrait of Moses." *Interpretation* 41/3 (1987): 245–55.

———. "The Prophetic Critique of Kings." *Ex Auditu* 2 (1986): 82–95.

Moscati, Sabatino, ed. *An Introduction to the Comparative Grammar of the Semitic Languages: Phonology and Morphology.* Wiesbaden: Otto Harrassowitz, 1980.

Moulton, J. H., and G. Milligan. *Vocabulary of the Greek Testament.* Peabody, Mass.: Hendrickson, 1930.

Mowinckel, Sigmund. *Psalmenstudien III: Kultprophetie und prophetische Psalmen.* Kristiana: Jacob Dybwad, 1923.

———. "The Spirit and the Word in Pre-exilic Reform Prophets." *JBL* 53 (1934): 199–227.

Origen. *On First Principles.* Translated by G. W. Butterworth. New York: Harper and Row, 1966.

Parker, T. H. L. *Calvin's Old Testament Commentaries.* Edinburgh: T. & T. Clark, 1986.

Petersen, David L. "Ecstasy and Role Enactment." In *The Place Is Too Small for Us: The Israelite Prophets in Recent*

Scholarship, edited by Robert P. Gordon, 279–88. Winona Lake, Ind.: Eisenbrauns, 1995.

Pritchard, James A. *Ancient Near Eastern Texts Relating to the Old Testament.* Princeton: Princeton University Press, 1969.

Reid, David P. *What Are They Saying about the Prophets?* New York: Paulist, 1980.

Rhodes, Arnold B. "Israel's Prophets as Intercessors." In *Scripture and Theology: Essays in Honor of J. Coert Rylaarsdam,* edited by Arthur L. Merrill and Thomas W. Overholt, 107–29. Pittsburgh: Pickwick, 1977.

Richards, Lawrence O., and Clyde Hoeldtke. *Church Leadership: Following the Example of Jesus Christ.* Grand Rapids: Zondervan, 1980.

Robinson, B. A. "How Many Wiccans Are There in the U.S.?" Cited 29 March 2002. Online: http://www.religioustolerance.org.

Robinson, H. Wheeler. *Corporate Personality in Ancient Israel.* 2d ed. Edinburgh: T. & T. Clark, 1981.

Rofé, Alexander. *Introduction to the Prophetic Literature.* Translated by Judith H. Seeligmann. Sheffield: Sheffield Academic Press, 1997.

Rowley, H. H. "The Nature of Prophecy in the Light of Recent Study." *HTR* 38 (1945): 1–38.

Ryken, Leland, James C. Wihoit, and Tremper Longman III, eds. *Dictionary of Biblical Imagery.* Downers Grove, Ill.: InterVarsity, 1998.

Savage, Peter. "The Church and Evangelicalism." In *The New Face of Evangelicalism,* edited by C. René Padilla, 106–20. Downers Grove, Ill.: InterVarsity, 1976.

Sawyer, John F. A. *Prophecy and the Biblical Prophets.* Oxford: Oxford University Press, 1993.

Scott, R. B. Y. *The Relevance of the Prophets.* New York: Macmillan, 1944.

Seilhamer, Frank H. *Prophets and Prophecy: Seven Key Messengers*. Philadelphia: Fortress, 1977.

Skillen, James W. "Prophecy, Critique, Action." *WTJ* 58 (1996): 85–110.

Smith, Gary V. *An Introduction to the Hebrew Prophets: The Prophets as Preachers*. Nashville: Broadman & Holman, 1994.

Snyder, Howard A. *The Community of the King*. Downers Grove, Ill.: InterVarsity, 1977.

Stacey, David. *Prophetic Drama in the Old Testament*. London: Epworth, 1990.

Terry, Milton S. *Biblical Hermeneutics: A Treatise on the Interpretation of the Old and New Testaments*. Grand Rapids: Zondervan, 1974.

Thiselton, Anthony C. *New Horizons in Hermeneutics: The Theory and Practice of Transforming Biblical Reading*. Grand Rapids: Zondervan, 1992.

Tucker, Gene. "Deuteronomy 18:15–22." *Interpretation* 41/3 (1987): 292–97.

———. "Prophetic Speech." In James L. Mays and Paul J. Achtemeier, eds., *Interpreting the Prophets*, 27–40. Philadelphia: Fortress, 1987.

VanGemeren, Willem A. *Interpreting the Prophetic Word: An Introduction to the Prophetic Literature of the Old Testament*. Grand Rapids: Zondervan, 1990.

———, ed. *New International Dictionary of Old Testament Theology and Exegesis*. 5 vols. Grand Rapids: Zondervan, 1997.

Volf, Miroslav. "The Church as a Prophetic Community and a Sign of Hope." *EuroJTh* 2/1 (1993): 9–30.

Von Rad, Gerhard. *Deuteronomy*. OTL. Philadelphia: Westminster, 1966.

Vos, Geerhardus. *Biblical Theology: Old and New Testaments*. Grand Rapids: Eerdmans, 1948.

Vriezen, Th. C. *An Outline of Old Testament Theology.* 2d ed. Oxford: Blackwell, 1970.

Wagner, E. Glenn. *Escape from Church, Inc.: The Return of the Pastor-Shepherd.* Grand Rapids: Zondervan, 1999.

Waltke, Bruce K., and M. O'Connor. *An Introduction to Biblical Hebrew Syntax.* Winona Lake, Ind.: Eisenbrauns, 1990.

Walton, John. *Ancient Israelite Literature in Its Cultural Context.* Chicago: Moody, 1992.

Ward, James M. *The Prophets.* Nashville: Abingdon, 1982.

———. *Thus Says the Lord: The Message of the Prophets,* Nashville: Abingdon, 1991.

Warren, Rick. *The Purpose-Driven Church: Growth Without Compromising Your Message and Mission.* Grand Rapids: Zondervan, 1995.

Watson, Gerard. "Origen and the Literal Interpretation of Scripture." In *Scriptural Interpretation in the Fathers: Letter and Spirit,* edited by Thomas Finan and Vincent Twomey, 75–84. Portland, Ore.: Four Courts, 1995.

Watts, John D. W. *Isaiah 1–33.* Word Biblical Commentary, vol. 24. Waco, Tex.: Word, 1985.

Westermann, Claus. *Basic Forms of Prophetic Speech.* Translated by Hugh Clayton White. Louisville: Westminster/John Knox, 1991.

Williams, Michael J. "An Investigation of the Legitimacy of Source Distinctions for the Prose Material in Jeremiah." *JBL* 112/2 (1993): 193–210.

Willis, John T. "Some Suggestions on the Interpretation of Micah 1:2." *VT* 18/3 (1968): 372–79.

Wilson, Robert R. "Early Israelite Prophecy." In James L. Mays and Paul J. Achtemeier, eds., *Interpreting the Prophets,* 1–13. Philadelphia: Fortress, 1987.

———. "Interpreting Israel's Religion: An Anthropological Perspective on the Problem of False Prophecy." In *The*

Place Is Too Small for Us: The Israelite Prophets in Recent Scholarship, edited by Robert P. Gordon, 332–44. Winona Lake, Ind.: Eisenbrauns, 1995.

———. *Prophecy and Society in Ancient Israel.* Philadelphia: Fortress, 1980.

Yoder, John Howard. "A People in the World: Theological Interpretation." In *The Concept of the Believers' Church,* edited by James L. Garrett Jr., 250–83. Scottdale, Pa.: Herald, 1967.

Young, Edward J. *My Servants the Prophets.* Grand Rapids: Eerdmans, 1952.

Zurick, David. *Errant Journeys: Adventure Travel in a Modern Age.* Austin: University of Texas Press, 1995.

INDEX OF SCRIPTURE

Index of Subjects
and Names

Michael J. Williams (M.A.R., Westminster Theological Seminary; Ph.D., University of Pennsylvania) is associate professor of Old Testament at Calvin Theological Seminary, where he has taught since 1995. He has also conducted lecture series in Kenya ("Old Testament Perspectives" for clergy in-service training) and the Ukraine ("The Prophetic Function of the Church").

Dr. Williams is author of *Deception in Genesis: An Investigation into the Morality of a Unique Biblical Phenomenon.* His articles have appeared in *Journal of Biblical Literature* and *Calvin Theological Journal,* and he has contributed to *The Oxford Dictionary of the Jewish Religion* and *The Dictionary of Biblical Imagery.*